Cambridge Elements ≡

Elements in the Problems of God
edited by
Michael L. Peterson
Asbury Theological Seminary

CHRISTIANITY AND THE PROBLEM OF FREE WILL

Leigh Vicens
Augustana University

CAMBRIDGE
UNIVERSITY PRESS

Shaftesbury Road, Cambridge CB2 8EA, United Kingdom

One Liberty Plaza, 20th Floor, New York, NY 10006, USA

477 Williamstown Road, Port Melbourne, VIC 3207, Australia

314–321, 3rd Floor, Plot 3, Splendor Forum, Jasola District Centre, New Delhi – 110025, India

103 Penang Road, #05–06/07, Visioncrest Commercial, Singapore 238467

Cambridge University Press is part of Cambridge University Press & Assessment, a department of the University of Cambridge.

We share the University's mission to contribute to society through the pursuit of education, learning and research at the highest international levels of excellence.

www.cambridge.org
Information on this title: www.cambridge.org/9781009270465

DOI: 10.1017/9781009270427

First published 2023

A catalogue record for this publication is available from the British Library.

ISBN 978-1-009-27046-5 Paperback
ISSN 2754-8724 (online)
ISSN 2754-8716 (print)

Cambridge University Press & Assessment has no responsibility for the persistence or accuracy of URLs for external or third-party internet websites referred to in this publication and does not guarantee that any content on such websites is, or will remain, accurate or appropriate.

Christianity and the Problem of Free Will

Elements in the Problems of God

DOI: 10.1017/9781009270427
First published online: May 2023

Leigh Vicens
Augustana University
Author for correspondence: Leigh Vicens, lvicens@augie.edu

Abstract: Central to the teachings of Christianity is a puzzle: on the one hand, sin seems something that humans do not do freely and so cannot be responsible for, since it is unavoidable; on the other hand, sin seems something that we must be responsible for and so do freely, since we are enjoined to repent of it, and since it makes us liable to divine condemnation and forgiveness. After laying out the puzzle in more depth, this Element considers three possible responses – libertarian, soft determinist, and free will skeptic – and weighs the costs and benefits of each.

Keywords: free will, sin, responsibility, Christianity, God

ISBNs: 9781009270465 (PB), 9781009270427 (OC)
ISSNs: 2754-8724 (online), 2754-8716 (print)

Contents

1 The Puzzle of Sin and Free Will

This Element grapples with a puzzle at the heart of Christian thought – a tension between claims that are central to Christian teaching. But what *is* the heart of Christian thought? What claims are central? Keith Yandell once proposed that what makes something a *religion* (and what distinguishes one religion from another) is that it offers a *diagnosis* – "an account of what it takes the basic problem facing human beings to be" – and a *cure* – "a way of permanently and desirably solving that problem" (1999, 17). Considered this way, we may get to the essence of Christianity by asking what it diagnoses and what it prescribes. Yandell characterizes Christianity thus: "The basic religious problem is sin, and the deepest religious need is for forgiveness," later clarifying that "Forgiveness is provided by God's grace or unmerited favor" (1999, 25).

Yandell's characterization, while sparse and absent some concepts central to the Gospel (e.g. justification, salvation, reconciliation – not to mention the Trinity, Incarnation, or Resurrection[1]), certainly gets at a key aspect of the Christian message: that we are sinners, and in need of forgiveness. Some Christian theologians have proposed that rather than beginning with an understanding of the basic human problem and looking to (Christian) religion to find a solution, we approach from the opposite direction, starting with Christ as cure in order to reveal what most deeply ails us.[2] If the good news is that through Christ we are *saved* (or justified, forgiven, or reconciled), then the fundamental problem is that we need salvation (or justification, forgiveness, or reconciliation). This answer then raises further questions: From what do we need to be saved – and why? For what do we need to be forgiven? Why do we need justification or reconciliation?

No matter which way we approach Christian thought – from what it diagnoses, or from what it prescribes – we end up, in characterizing Christianity, making essential reference to the concept of *sin*. And it is the New Testament's conception of sin, and its relationship to other concepts such as human agency, autonomy, and responsibility, that generate a puzzle.[3] The puzzle may be put

---

[1] Some of these concepts feature in Yandell's lengthier characterization.

[2] Douglass Moo summarizes the scholarship of E. P. Sanders, who argued that "Paul's theological reasoning moved 'from solution to plight'," reassessing "the nature of humanity's problem" on the basis of his experience of "the good news of God's intervention on behalf of humanity in Christ" (Moo 2013, 108). Moo reports that "Sanders's 'solution to plight' analysis of Paul's theology has been widely accepted" (Moo 2013, 108).

[3] The reader may notice that we move below from a focus on "the heart of Christian thought" or claims "central to Christianity" to consideration of various passages of the New Testament. But what is the relationship between Christian teaching and biblical texts? The answer to this question is complicated and could take an entire book to explore. Suffice to say here, Christians interpret the New Testament in light of creedal statements, ecumenical declarations, and other historical documents, even as these pronouncements themselves reflect interpretations of biblical texts.

succinctly as follows: on the one hand, sin seems like something that we do not do freely, and so something for which we cannot be responsible; on the other hand, sin seems like something for which we *must* be responsible, and so something which we indeed do freely.

The reason that our sin seems unfree is that, according to the New Testament, sin is *unavoidable* for humans (apart from Christ). We may see this by starting either with biblical portrayals of sin, or with the evident universal need of salvation (or justification, forgiveness, or reconciliation). To start with the prescriptive end, Jesus even before his birth is portrayed as one who will save people *from their sins* (Matt. 1:21) and by forgiveness *of their sins* (Luke 1:77); he is the one who "takes away the sin of the world" (John 1:29), who was made "to be sin . . . so that in him we might become the righteousness of God" (2 Cor. 5:21).[4] Unless we think that some human beings are not in need of salvation, or can save themselves from sin – possibilities that the New Testament unequivocally rules out (1 Tim. 4:10: "we have our hope set on the living God, who is the Saviour of *all* people"; Acts 4:12: "there is salvation in *no one else*; Ephesians 2:8: For by grace you have been saved through faith, and *this is not your own doing*") – then we must admit that *all* are sinners; sin is a universal human problem. And, indeed, this is precisely what the New Testament writers are at pains to emphasize (see Romans 3:23; 1 John 1:8).

Moreover, turning to the diagnosis, or biblical characterization of our fundamental problem, sin seems not simply something we happen to commit but might have avoided; rather, sin exercises a kind of "dominion" over all of us (Romans 5:14, 6:12, 6:14), against which we are (or were, before being saved) helpless. Paul likens being "under" sin both to being a slave (Romans 6:6, 6:17, 6:20, 7:14, 7:25; see also John 8:34) – a paradigmatically *unfree* person – and to being dead (Ephesians 2:1, 2:5; Romans 6:13); and if there is anyone who is less free than a slave, it is a dead person! In his letter to the Romans, Paul personifies sin as a "power" who "dwells" within him, holding him "captive" and making him do what he does not want to do (3:9; 7:19, 7:20, 7:23); here as in other places, Paul seems to be describing a universal human condition when he writes, "Wretched man that I am! Who will rescue me from this body of death? Thanks be to God through Jesus Christ our Lord!" (Romans 7:26–27). Thus again the human condition is revealed through the nature of our salvation: Christ is the liberator and life-giver (see Moo 2013).

While there are thus many sources one could explore in consideration of the fundamentals of Christian teaching, this book focuses mainly on the New Testament, because the puzzle of sin and free will stands in such sharp relief in its pages.

[4] Throughout this book, biblical quotations are from the *New Revised Standard Version*, and all emphases are added.

Finally, there is the idea, suggested in the New Testament and developed by the Christian tradition, that each individual does not independently fall prey to this same power at some point in their lives. Rather, we are all *born into* sin, in the sense that our nature is corrupted in a way that makes sin inevitable for each of us. And our sins are all connected and in some way explained by the "original" sin of the first human sinner, Adam. The doctrine of original sin will be explored further in the next section.

Of course, the idea that we are not free with respect to sin might be resisted, and we will consider in depth some attempts to defend human freedom with respect to sin later in this Element. For now, we consider the other New Testament idea that seems to be in tension with this one: that sin is something for which we are responsible. One easy route to this conclusion is to note the frequent language of divine *judgment* against sinners. The New Testament characterizes all humans, on account of their sins, as liable to condemnation and wrath, and saved only through the grace of God. Paul even describes the salvation wrought through Christ's death as salvation "from the wrath of God" (Romans 5:9), and Christ as the one "who rescues us from the wrath" (1 Thess. 1:10). And it is sin that brings condemnation; indeed, Paul writes that the very sin (Adam's) that apparently makes sin inevitable for the rest of us "led to condemnation for all" (Romans 5:18). Our universal condemnation is traditionally understood not (only) as condemnation for Adam's sin, but as condemnation for our own sin, which Adam's sin makes inevitable. Besides condemnation and wrath, Paul describes humans as liable to "recompense for what has been done in the body, whether good or evil" (2 Cor. 5), "vengeance," and "the punishment of eternal destruction" for not knowing God and not obeying the gospel (2 Thess. 1:8–9). If there is any question about the justice of God's directing his wrath against helpless sinners, Paul is at pains to clarify: "what should we say? That God is unjust to inflict wrath on us? (I speak in a human way.) By no means!" (Romans 3:5).

And themes of divine judgment are found not only in Pauline epistles. John says that those who do not believe in the Son "are condemned already" (3:18) and that "whoever disobeys the Son will not see life, but must endure God's wrath" (3:36), while in Matthew's Gospel, Jesus counsels, "If your right eye causes you to sin, tear it out and throw it away; it is better for you to lose one of your members than for your whole body to be thrown into hell" (5:29; see also Mark 9:43–48). The language of judgment, condemnation, wrath, and (eternal) punishment all strongly suggest that we are *responsible* for our sin. And free will is normally understood as a requirement for responsibility – that is, we are only responsible for what we do, or how we are, insofar as we do it or are that way freely, or at least, freely did something in the past which led to our present state (Wolf 1990; Fischer 1994; Ekstrom 2000; Mele 2006; Levy 2011; Pereboom 2014).

Another route to get to this second idea, that sin is something we do freely and for which we are responsible, is to focus on the New Testament injunction to *repent*. Repentance is an early and consistent theme in Jesus's preaching (see, for example, Matt 4:17), involves turning away from one's sins (and toward God), and is tied to forgiveness. Jesus tells his disciples, "repentance and forgiveness of sins is to be proclaimed in [the Messiah's] name to all nations" (Luke 24:47), while Peter commands the crowds to "repent . . . and turn to God so that your sins may be wiped out" (Acts 3:19). But a person's repenting from sin implies that she is responsible for sin – and so again, that she sinned freely.

A third, related route to our apparent freedom and responsibility with respect to sin is based on the New Testament theme of forgiveness of sins, which, as noted above, is central to the Gospel (see also Acts 2:38, Col. 1:14, Ephesians 4:32, 1 John 1:9). Forgiveness is distinguished from excuse on the basis of responsibility ascriptions. I may excuse you for pushing me in a crowd of people when I realize that you yourself were pushed and couldn't help but push me in turn; in excusing you, I thereby acknowledge that you were not really responsible for what you did. Forgiving you, in contrast, would seem to require taking you to be responsible for pushing me (Hieronymi 2001; Garrard and McNaughton 2010; Strabbing 2017; Warmke, Nelkin, and McKenna 2021). Thus God's forgiveness of our sins would also seem to require that we are responsible for those sins (Capes 2022).

And so we have a puzzle to solve! Of course, there are quite a number of puzzles in the New Testament – how God can be one, if three persons; how Jesus can be both fully God and fully human; why an omnipotent and perfectly good God would allow evil in the world – and a common approach to these apparent contradictions is simply to throw up one's hands and declare them divine mysteries. Indeed, we might think that this is the best or only way to respect the authority of Scripture and the inscrutability of God (see Romans 11:33).[5] Yet the puzzle here seems importantly different than other theological puzzles to which this type of response is often directed: for the puzzle here is not simply or primarily about the nature or mind of *God*, but about *our own* nature and capacities. It is a puzzle about human agency and responsibility, and so solving it, or at least making some attempt at considering possible responses, seems important to our own self-understanding.

---

[5] Another possibility is simply to accept that the New Testament contains a contradiction. Not many have gone this route, though some theologians describe *sin* as a "surd." See, for instance, Tanner (1994, 112) and Burrell (2008, 186).

In what follows, therefore, I consider three types of responses to the puzzle of sin and free will. In Section 2, I approach the puzzle from a *libertarian* stance – roughly, from the position that our free will with respect to sin requires our ability to do otherwise than sin and so is incompatible with our being determined to sin. In Section 3, I look at what might be said by a *soft determinist* – one who accepts that we are determined to sin, and yet insists that our free will and responsibility for sin are compatible with this determinism. And in Section 4, I consider the perspective of those who accept the unavoidability of sin but are *skeptics* about free will. I intend to show that none of these responses to the puzzle is completely without costs, in terms of naturally interpreting biblical passages and maintaining theological doctrine (and common sense). In the fourth and final section I propose what I take to be the least costly resolution to the problem, which might be located somewhere between free will skepticism and compatibilism about free will and determinism.

2 Libertarian Solutions
Introducing Libertarianism

Many respond to the puzzle presented in the previous section by insisting that free will is a non-negotiable feature of the biblical picture of humanity – and of our life experiences and practices.[6] So if our free will is in conflict with the unavoidability of sin, then so much the worse for the unavoidability of sin! But why think the unavoidability of sin is in conflict with free will, anyway? One intuitive answer is that free will involves the *ability to do otherwise*: it requires having at least two options, and being able to bring about either option (see van Inwagen, 2008). But if sin is unavoidable for me, then I have no other option than to sin – or, if I do have another option, I do not have the ability to bring it about. A second, related answer is that if sin is unavoidable for me, then I must be determined to sin – that is, my sin must be necessitated by something else, so that given this "something else," I had to sin. But being determined or necessitated in this way is incompatible with being free. The idea that free will is incompatible with being completely determined in one's actions is called *incompatibilism* – as opposed to *compatibilism*, the idea that determinism doesn't rule out one's being free. The view that free will exists and is incompatible with determinism is called *libertarianism*. Many libertarians (called "leeway incompatibilists" – see Timpe 2007) hold a view of free will as the ability to do otherwise, though some ("source incompatibilists") maintain that free will is about being the ultimate source of one's actions, which, while ruling out

---

[6] Much of this chapter develops arguments first presented in Vicens (2022b).

determinism, may or may not require the ability to do otherwise (see Tognazzini 2011).

Why be a libertarian? Since libertarianism is a combination of two theses – the *existence* of free will and the *incompatibility* of free will and determinism – it will require reasons supporting each of these theses. In the previous section we saw biblical reasons for the existence thesis: free will seems required for moral responsibility, and so divine condemnation and forgiveness, as well as human repentance, which are all central themes of the New Testament. Moreover, setting aside the biblical evidence and divine–human relations, if free will is required for moral responsibility, then it will be essential to our holding *each other* responsible as well, from the attitudes involved in human relationships – gratitude, anger, guilt, forgiveness, etc. – which seem to have assumptions of responsibility "built in" to them (see Strawson 1963), to practices of punishment and reward. Free will also seems to many like something we can "read off" of our experience, and that grounds our everyday processes of deliberation and decision (van Inwagen 1983) as well as our creative acts.

But why be an incompatibilist about free will and determinism? Most of the reasoning here is more philosophical and technical, though some take incompatibilism to be a deep-seated intuition, and others think that not only the existence of free will but the existence of indeterminism is presumed in our making choices or can be read off of our experience of choice. Laura Ekstrom, for instance, maintains that "we regard the future as including alternatives that are open to us" in the sense of "genuinely available forking paths" (2021, 64), and Robert Kane has likened our sense of our own agency to Jorge Luis Borges's "garden of forking paths" (2005, 7). Kane's own developed view of free will, based in part on this sense of agency, is of a power to literally create the self, by acting so as to "form one's own will in a manner that is undetermined by one's past" (2005, 172).[7]

One of the most common types of arguments for incompatibilism is the Consequence Argument, which begins with the fact that if an action is determined by something other than the agent acting then *what determines the agent's action* is not under the agent's control, and concludes that neither is the *action itself* under the agent's control (see van Inwagen 1983; Vicens 2012b; Finch 2022). For example, suppose a person's violent behavior on a certain occasion is completely determined by some combination of factors including his genetics and early childhood experiences of abuse and neglect (among many other factors including the situation at the time of the violent episode). What it

---

[7] See also Searle (1984, 95) and O'Connor (1995, 196–197) for the view that our experience of our own free choice is evidence for libertarianism.

means for his behavior to be determined by these factors is that it *had* to happen, given the occurrence of these factors, or in other words, that his behavior could *not* have been prevented, unless at least some of these factors had been prevented. Now we might think that these determining factors did not themselves all have to happen – it was not absolutely necessary that the person was neglected or abused, say. But the point is that the person himself did not have control over whether he was neglected or abused at such a young age – nor did he have control over his genes, or the way in which this confluence of factors influenced his behavior (by assumption: for if he did have control over this influence, then his behavior wouldn't be determined). And so we may conclude that he did not have control over the behavior itself; and so he cannot be considered free with respect to, or responsible for, his violent behavior. A second type of argument for incompatibilism is the Manipulation Argument, which depends on the premise that there is no relevant difference between factors that preclude an agent's acting freely – in particular, manipulation by another agent – and determination of the agent's action by something other than the agent herself (see Pereboom 2001, 110–117; Mele 2006, 184–195). Finally, as we will see in the next section in considering difficulties faced by compatibilism, there may be distinctly theological reasons in favor of incompatibilism, having to do with God's lack of responsibility for human sin, and God's standing to blame and punish.

Sin as Almost Unavoidable

Returning to our puzzle we may ask, how can the libertarian make sense of the apparent unavoidability of sin as presented in the New Testament? One way would be to understand sin as *for all intents and purposes* universal and inevitable, while still leaving open the possibility of an individual's not sinning. Richard Swinburne, for instance, describes human sin as "pervasive" and "almost unavoidable" (1989, 146), while Thomas Talbott offers an account of the "near universality and seeming inevitability of human sin" which "virtually guarantees" that individuals will sin (2008, 306–7). I see two sub-options here. The first would be to emphasize the fact that we each have many opportunities to sin, given the length of our lives and the extent of our free will. Even if it's not highly likely that I will sin on any particular occasion, still, given enough occasions, it is highly likely that I will sin eventually. Consider, on analogy, that if I flip a fair coin once, it is not highly likely that it will come up heads: the probability is only 50 percent. But if I flip the coin ten times, the probability that it will come up heads at least once becomes 99.9 percent. And presumably, we have many more than ten chances to sin! And so, while the probability that each individual sins isn't exactly 100 percent, it is approximately so.[8]

The main problem with this picture should be obvious: while it is highly likely that each individual will sin, it is not guaranteed. And while the more opportunities an individual has to sin, the greater the probability that she will sin eventually, the more individuals there are, the greater the chances that one of them will *not* sin. But the New Testament authors speak as though the universality of sin is a foregone conclusion, not something that is simply highly likely. And the possibility – however unlikely – that someone (apart from Christ) will be sinless would seem to obviate the necessity of a universal Savior from sin. Relatedly, this probabilistic picture doesn't seem to match the New Testament portrayal of sin discussed in the previous section, as a kind of power that has dominion over us, making us like slaves in need of liberation, or dead people in need of new life.

The second sub-option would be to say that it is not only that we are very likely to sin at some point in our lives, but that there are many so-called near occasions for sin when sin is very likely. The high probability may be explained in terms of our disordered desires, warped attitudes, or self-interested motivations, and the difficulty that we face in overcoming them to avoid sin on any given occasion. This seems to be the position of both Swinburne and Talbott; Swinburne writes of our strong selfish desires (1989, 112) that "incline" us to sin (1989, 138) and amount to a "proneness to objective wrongdoing" (1989, 112), while Talbott describes our early childhood context as one of "ambiguity, ignorance, and misperception" that, in combination with our natural instincts, "comes close to guaranteeing ... that we would repeatedly 'miss the mark'" (2008, 306).

Of course, there is still the possibility that some individual may "beat the odds" and avoid sin on every occasion, making a person sinless and in no need of salvation from sin – though perhaps it better accounts for the biblical characterizations of sin as a force to be reckoned with. However, this view faces an additional difficulty. For it would seem that if determinism completely eliminates the possibility of free will and moral responsibility, then, the closer one gets to determinism, the more diminished one's free will and moral responsibility are. If, given factors over which one has (had) no control, one is 99.999999 percent likely to sin on a given occasion, one would seem to be less blameworthy for sinning than if one is, say, 50 percent likely. Philip Swenson (2021), in attempting to solve the problem of moral luck, presents

---

[8] Some authors seem to think that even if sin is not unavoidable for an individual on any particular occasion, it may be unavoidable (and not simply *almost* unavoidable) over the course of the individual's life. For a critique of this idea, see Franks (2012) and Vicens (2022b).

a view according to which a person is less blameworthy for moral wrongdoing the less likely she is (through no fault of her own) to avoid moral wrongdoing. The problem is that on this view, if an individual is, through no fault of her own, *virtually guaranteed* to sin, then she will be *virtually blameless* for doing so. But a main motivation for maintaining libertarianism, as mentioned already, is to make sense of the biblical language of divine judgment of sin, including *condemnation*, *wrath*, and *hell*. And no one could be deserving of hell unless her blameworthiness were "turned up to the maximum," so to speak. So the idea that we are by nature very inclined to sin without being strictly necessitated to do so seems to undermine a central theological motivation for maintaining libertarianism.

Guaranteeing Sin through Middle Knowledge

We have been working under the assumption that if it is *guaranteed* that a person will sin, then that person must be *determined* to sin – and so, to avoid this deterministic conclusion, we have considered the possibility that a person's sinning is not absolutely guaranteed but simply very likely. But some would question our starting assumption: Why think that something cannot be guaranteed to happen unless it is determined? Couldn't there be some facts about what a person will do – facts that could be known by an omniscient God – even if the person has the ability to do otherwise? Such knowledge – called "simple foreknowledge" – would allow the possessor assurance that all created persons with libertarian freedom will in fact sin, and so will be in need of salvation from sin. Of course, simple foreknowledge would be in an important sense "after the fact": God would not know that I *will in fact* sin in my life until deciding to create me, in the circumstances in which I will sin. But God might have another type of knowledge – knowledge before deciding to create a person – of what she *would* do, *were* God to create her in particular circum-stances. This knowledge is *counterfactual* knowledge, since it needn't be about the actual world – after all, God might decide not to create the person, or not to put her in the circumstances in which she would sin. Luis de Molina dubbed such knowledge "middle knowledge" since it is *in between* God's "natural" knowledge (of necessary truths), and "free" knowledge (of contingent truths which He determines). Middle knowledge is knowledge of contingent truths, the truth value of which is up to (possible) free creatures and not God (see Freddoso 1988; Flint 1998).

Middle knowledge might help us make sense of the unavoidability of sin. For God might know, even before creating the actual world, that each of the people He will create, if given significant freedom (freedom to choose between good and evil), will sin at some point in their lives. In fact, God might even know that, for any person He might create, if He created them with significant freedom, they would sin at some point in their lives – this is Alvin Plantinga's (1974) thesis of "transworld depravity." Neither universal sin nor transworld depravity can be explained by the fact that actual or possible people are determined to sin, say Molinists (defenders of middle knowledge); rather, such people have the ability to do otherwise, but God knows that they will not do otherwise if given the opportunity. So Molinists can maintain both the unavoidability of sin, and the existence of (libertarian) free will with respect to sin. Or so they say!

However, serious objections have been raised to the metaphysical possibility of middle knowledge, or the idea that there could be counterfactuals of libertarian freedom. According to the "grounding" objection, for instance, there is nothing that could ground counterfactuals of libertarian freedom, or make them true, since the individuals they are about might never exist or be in the circumstances they describe; and these "facts" are not supposed to be determined by anything except the individuals themselves (see Adams 1977; Hasker 1989).

While we will not get into the details of such objections, the doctrine of middle knowledge also seems unable to answer a question relevant to the issue under consideration here: *Why* do all (actual or possible) people sin? As Hugh McCann and Daniel Johnson note, on the "standard" (libertarian) view, it "can only be a mystery" why, "although all of us possess libertarian freedom, and so have the option of serving God, still *all* humans sin" – as if "God suffers a terrible run of bad luck in a grand lottery of his own institution," in finding that every actual or possible person He does or could create would sin at least once if given the chance (2017). This seems unproblematic for the purpose for which Plantinga originally proposed the transworld depravity thesis: as a thesis which is *possibly* true (or, rather, a thesis about what is possible) about the options God faced at creation; for Plantinga was only trying to show that the existence of evil is not logically incompatible with the existence of a perfect God. But here we are considering not merely what is possible, but what we know (or at least are supposing) to be true: that sin is universal and inevitable for all created persons, such that all are in need of salvation. But then both transworld and actual-world depravity seem inexplicable and implausible. And as noted already, the New Testament does not present the universality of sin as an odd coincidence, but a reality predicted and explained by certain more fundamental facts about sin and human nature. As I have put the point elsewhere, while God's knowledge of transworld or actual-world depravity might give us a guarantee of the brute fact of sin's *universality*, the New Testament tells of sin's *unavoidability* due to its *mastery* over us (Vicens 2022b).

Responsibility for Counterfactual Sin

Mark B. Anderson has recently made a different kind of appeal to middle knowledge, in an attempt to account for the Christian idea that *all* created persons – even infants and young children – are blameworthy. "How can we be deserving of condemnation before we even develop as moral agents?" he asks (2021, 5) – and how can it be, even among mature adults, that "All are equally guilty, equally in desperate need of God's grace" given the evident fact that "there seems to be a stark moral difference between a Gandhi and a Pol Pot" (2021, 19)? Rather than insisting that all of us actually use our free will to sin, Anderson suggests that all of us *would* sin, in some situation or other – and our "true moral responsibility" hinges upon not only what we in fact do, but "what we would have done if things were different" (2021, 11) – in other words, on counterfactuals of libertarian freedom. While we like to think that, had we been in Germany in the 1930s and 1940s, we would have sided with the resistance and not the Nazis, Anderson suggests that we should not be so sure. And while a young child might be innocent of any actual sin, we may consider her as much a helpless wretch as the rest of us, "because the counterfactuals that describe . . . her will were true long before . . . her birth" (2021, 16) – and some of them describe sin that she would commit if given the chance.

Anderson admits to the radical nature of this proposal: "We are talking about a perspective according to which what you would have done as a Cro-Magnon in the Paleolithic Age counts every bit as much toward your degree of responsibility as what you actually do during the course of your life. Such a thesis is bound to provoke an incredulous stare" (2021, 12). And yet, he notes that the view can deal with the problem of moral luck – how it could be fair to hold us responsible for our morally good or bad actions or traits, given the evident influence of factors like genetics, upbringing, and social factors on our (im)moral behavior and the obvious fact that some of us are luckier than others in terms of the factors that influence – as alternative views cannot:

> For those who deny that there can be true counterfactuals of libertarian freedom, a complete description of an agent's will cannot extend beyond the confines of the actual world – and so it is riddled with the impurities of luck, which create the traction of circumstances against which that will is exercised. But for the Molinist, the complete description of the agent's will must include a great library of true counterfactuals of libertarian freedom which, taken in total, eliminate those impurities. What is left is the naked will. If that naked will becomes the object of our evaluation, then it is me and me *alone* that is on the scales of justice – not the circumstances of my birth, not my neurological makeup, not the culture in which I was raised, nor any other feature of me external to my will. (2021, 15)

Anderson's proposal is a stunning one, and for those troubled by moral luck, it seems deeply satisfying. But the costs to this view are steep as well. First, as mentioned above, there are substantial objections to the theory of middle knowledge. Then there is the very strong conception of free will and personal identity expressed in the above passage. While moral luck has been eradicated, the pendulum seems to have swung too far in the opposite direction, in supposing that the most important facts about us – the facts that will matter in God's final judgment of our ultimate worth and desert – pertain to our "naked will," a will stripped of all such "external" features as our genetics and upbringing. Yet one might wonder how there could be anything, or at least *so much* of significance, left once these features are stripped away.

Relatedly, on Anderson's proposal, we are not able to do a comparative moral evaluation of the likes of Gandhi and Pol Pot. There is no knowing what each would have done in the other's shoes: perhaps Gandhi would have left a murderous legacy in radically different (Pol Pot-esque) circumstances. And yet, while we have already noted that the Molinist seems to lack an explanation for the universality of sin (in the actual world or across possible worlds),[9] the idea that under different circumstances, the saintly Gandhi might have been a monstrous sinner seems to cry out for a (deterministic) explanation that appeals to those very circumstances – an explanation that is off limits for the Molinist.

Finally, there is an objection that Anderson himself considers, which he puts in terms of reconciliation with God, but which we might instead put in terms of sanctification: What could the sanctified life, or sanctified selves, look like on this view? Returning to the biblical picture of salvation considered in the previous section – Christ as liberator of captives, or life-giver to the dead – we may recall that the good news is that God will save us from our condition as wretched sinners, and transform us into saints, purifying us so that in heaven we (can) no longer sin. But as Anderson notes, counterfactuals of freedom cannot be changed, even by God: "A fallen condition can be cured; depraved counterfactuals of libertarian freedom cannot" (2021, 21). Anderson proposes, as a solution to this problem, that rather than transform our nature, God in heaven "severely delimit[s] the range of any possible future circumstances. A certain counterfactual purity may yet hold within that narrower range of circumstances,

---

[9] Anderson insists (personal communication) that he *does* provide an explanation for the universality of sin: one that appeals to the indefinitely many counterfactual situations in which we each might sin, and the unlikelihood that any of us remain sinless in all of them. I take this to be a version of the probabilistic response considered earlier in this chapter – though perhaps given that a person counterfactually has infinitely many and not simply a large finite number of opportunities to sin, this view does not amount to a "virtual" guarantee that everyone will sin, but an *actual* guarantee.

despite the fact that we may be thoroughly depraved outside of it. Because of God's activity, however, we would never sin in any future scenario that is possible relative to that activity" (2021, 22).

But delimiting the range of our circumstances to prevent us from committing the sin that we otherwise would commit seems a far cry from the picture of sanctification presented by the New Testament, in which our old self is crucified with Christ "so that the body of sin might be destroyed" (Romans 6:6). Paul's view sounds little like God changing our circumstances, and more like God changing our very selves, so that Christ is "formed" in us (Galatians 4:20) and comes to "live" in us (Galatians 2:20). And other New Testament authors concur: John describes the process of sanctification as being cleansed from all unrighteousness (1 John 1:9), Peter as becoming "participants of the divine nature" (2 Peter 1:4) and the author of Hebrews as simply being "perfected for all time" (10:14). To point the point differently, God's action in and through us in putting to death our sinful selves and raising us to life in Christ, as perfected persons and participants of God's nature, sounds not at all like preserving our "naked will" and sheltering it from circumstances of temptation, but rather like completely remaking our will from the ground up.[10]

Tracing Responsibility to an Original Free Choice

In attempting to account for the universality and inevitability of sin, we have been dancing around the historical idea of *original sin*. While there is no single agreed-upon doctrine of original sin across Christian traditions, in western Christendom St. Augustine's views have been influential. Augustine was himself inspired by the writings of St. Paul, who in his letter to the Romans set up a parallel and contrast between Adam's sin and Christ's righteousness: "just as one man's trespass led to condemnation for all, so one man's act of righteousness leads to justification and life for all. For just as by the one man's disobedience the many were made sinners, so by the one man's obedience the many will be made righteous" (5:18–19). Two ideas central to Augustine's thinking are *original guilt* and *constitutional fault* (Timpe 2021; see also Rea 2007; Crisp 2009; Quinn 2010). The former means that all people are born guilty because of the sin of the first man, Adam; the latter means that because of that first sin, all are born into a corrupted state that makes further sin inevitable for everyone.

---

[10] Of course, if a change in circumstances, as Anderson understands it, includes everything except a change in the "naked will," then God can keep us from sinning through quite significant modifications to our "constitutive features" – by altering our neural wiring or our genetic code or other deep aspects of our makeup (Anderson, personal communication). Perhaps this deals with the problem of sanctification, though to my mind it accentuates the implausibility of this view of the will and personal identity.

Both of these ideas are prima facie incompatible with libertarianism. We have already considered various libertarian attempts to make sense of something like constitutional fault, which requires that an individual is determined to sin by something (in this case, Adam's sin) over which she would seem to have no control – which, according to the Consequence Argument, entails that the individual has no control over her own sin either. And original guilt seems even more directly in conflict with libertarianism, since it posits that each individual is responsible for Adam's sin itself. But some libertarians have maintained that, appearances notwithstanding, we all really did have control over Adam's sin, having participated in it ourselves. Oliver Crisp explains that on an "Augustinian realist" interpretation of original sin, "Adam's sin and guilt ... is (somehow) *really* mine" (2009, 437). Different realists account for this "somehow" in different ways. Crisp (in 2009) favors a view according to which Adam and his heirs are members of one entity that persists through time; and "like an acorn that is infected with some disease that then affects all the later stages in the life of the sapling and tree into which it grows," so we later parts of the entity *fallen humanity* are transmitted Adam's "morally vitiated condition" by divine arrangement (2009, 439). Michael Rea, in contrast, considers a theory according to which Adam and his posterity are distinct individuals who shared a common temporal state and who underwent fission at the time of Adam's first sin, splitting into all the people who have ever lived or will (2007, 334).[11]

How one evaluates such an explanation for the inevitability of sin would seem to depend a lot on one's starting point. Rea suggests that the metaphysical commitments of fission theory come at "too high a price" (2007, 345), but Crisp appears to think otherwise. Though he admits that his favored version of Augustinian realism is "strong mead that may be difficult to swallow," Crisp writes, "the problems of the transmission of Adam's sin (and guilt) ... are theological difficulties at the heart of the Christian faith that many of the greatest minds in Christendom have struggled to overcome" (2009, 443–444).[12] He thus suggests that the difficulties associated with Augustinian realism are balanced out by their ability to solve such intractable theological puzzles. But it should be noted that the difficulty Crisp is attempting to overcome is generated in large part by a starting assumption of libertarianism.

---

[11] An alternative interpretation of original sin is the "federalist" view on which Adam was a representative of all of humanity in a way that made all humans responsible for his act of rebellion against God – much like citizens of a country would be responsible for their political leader's act of war. While this view would make sense of original guilt, it would not help with constitutional fault, and so would leave us with the puzzle of why sin is inevitable for all humans; for this reason it will be set aside.

[12] In later work such as (2020), Crisp repudiates the aspect of this view according to which all humans are guilty of Adam's sin.

There would be no puzzle requiring fission or four-dimensionalism to account for constitutional fault, at least, without the assumption that an individual cannot be determined to sin (culpably) by something over which she has no control. Compatibilists would have no difficulty affirming with Paul that "by the one man's disobedience the many were made sinners"; for compatibilists allow that we may be free and responsible for our sins even if our sins are determined by factors (including the sins of our forebearers) over which we have no control.[13] While giving up incompatibilism might seem a serious cost, it must be weighed against the costs of accepting that each of us somehow participated in the sin of the first human.

Even setting aside the metaphysical costs specific to Augustinian realism, there are other difficulties associated with Augustine's doctrine of original sin. As Swinburne notes, Christians in the first few centuries after Christ did not hold such a high view of Adam, according to which he was "a perfect man without proneness to sin"; rather, on their view, "Adam was a feeble creature," childlike in his cognitive and moral capacities (1989, 141). Swinburne argues that this earlier view of Adam is more in accord with evolutionary theory, suggesting as it does "a very gradual evolution of man from more primitive creatures with a very gradual developing of his various capacities" (1989, 141–142). Thomas Talbott further argues that the early Christian view of the first sin – a "consequence of the unperfected condition in which our first parents initially emerged and started making choices" – comports well with the biblical account of Adam and Eve in both Genesis and the New Testament, who came into being "with no clear understanding of good and evil" (2008, 310). But if Adam's choice to once disobey God brought immediate condemnation to all his progeny (of the sort to make them liable to damnation) as Augustine thought, then Adam's responsibility – and so, his moral capacities – must have been maximal.[14] This is all to say that if, in an attempt to account for the inevitability

---

[13] What about original guilt? This doctrine seems as difficult to make sense of by a compatibilist as by a libertarian, for neither allows that we could be responsible for *someone else's* sin. But Crisp argues in a later article that original guilt is not among the "core tenets common to all historic, orthodox doctrines of original sin" (2015, 257); and as Timpe notes, "the Catholic tradition" and "many of the Orthodox traditions" reject original guilt as well (2021). And neither does it seem entailed by the passage from Romans quoted earlier; for the condemnation for all to which Adam's trespass led may be condemnation not for Adam's trespass, but for our own sins, which Adam's trespass has made inevitable.

[14] Katherin Rogers seems to miss this point, when, responding to Marilyn McCord Adam's contention that Adam and Eve could not be fully responsible for their choice, given their partial ignorance of the consequences, Rogers writes, "Perhaps the Augustinian can agree with Adams that if Adam and Eve had actually understood and intended to produce the results which the Augustinian tradition ascribes to the fall, then they should be judged even *more* responsible [or guilty] .... Nonetheless ... it is enough that the tradition hold the first people *sufficiently* responsible, and for that, in the Augustinian view, all that is required is that they knowingly chose

of sin from a libertarian perspective, one appeals to Augustine's view of original sin, one should note the costs, not only of the realist interpretation of that doctrine which seems required by libertarianism, but also of the anti-evolutionary bent of Augustine's view. And while it might seem like the fall of a perfectly righteous man is the only possible reading of Scripture, other interpretations have dominated in different periods of Christian history. These comments are meant not to completely rule out of consideration an Augustinian take on original sin, but to motivate consideration of alternative accounts of the unavoidability of human sin, to which we turn in the next two sections.

3 Soft Determinist Solutions

Introducing Soft Determinism

In the previous section, we considered how *libertarians* – those who believe that free will exists and is incompatible with determinism (and so, determinism is false) – account for the inevitability of sin. In this section, we approach the puzzle of sin and free will from the perspective of those who believe that free will exists and yet determinism is *true*. The view that free will and determinism are compatible we have called *compatibilism*. And, historically, the view that determinism is true and free will actually exists has been called *soft determinism*, to distinguish it from the "hard" view that determinism is true and rules out the existence of free will.

Why be a soft determinist or a compatibilist? Since soft determinism, like libertarianism, is the combination of multiple theses, we will have to consider multiple different kinds of arguments for the view. One way of thinking is that free will quite evidently exists – we may again appeal to the phenomenology of agency, or the necessity of free will for some essential thing like moral responsibility – and that evidence supports the truth of determinism of one form or another, whether at the microphysical level of quantum physics, the biological level of genetics, or the social level, in the way our upbringing or environmental factors affect our behavior.[15] While some find incompatibilism to be the natural position, others argue, and support their argument with empirical research, that most people find compatibilism to be more intuitive (Nahmias and Murray 2010), and so compatibilism should be the default position in the absence of strong arguments against it. Compatibilists also raise objections to the arguments mentioned in the previous

---

disobedience to God" (2002, 72). But if you are not maximally guilty, then you would not seem liable to the kind of blanket condemnation, wrath, and punishment that have, following Augustine, been understood as deserved by all human beings on account of Adam's sin.

[15] Philosophers don't tend to take this approach, because of the difficulty of establishing that *all* human behavior (and, indeed, *every event*) is determined.

section in support of incompatibilism[16] and to the assumption that moral responsibility requires alternative possibilities which are themselves incompatible with determinism. Harry Frankfurt (1969) has offered a thought experiment in which a person seems to act of his own free will, even though, unbeknownst to him, another agent has closed off all possibilities of his doing otherwise. Frankfurt and other compatibilists have also developed accounts of free will that seem independently plausible and are compatible with determinism. On Frankfurt's "hierarchical" view, for instance, a person is free when she has the will that she wants to have, in the sense that she acts on a desire that she reflectively endorses (Frankfurt 1971).[17] Frankfurt shows that an agent can meet this criterion for being free even if she is determined. Some even argue that moral responsibility *requires* determinism, since indeterminism involved in choice would amount to mere randomness and so undermine control (Ayer 1954). Finally, while we may be uncertain about the current evidence in support of determinism, some maintain that the discovery of determinism in quantum physics or the like would do nothing to undermine our commitment to human freedom or moral responsibility (Fischer 2006).

In addition to these philosophical and empirical considerations, there are also distinctly theological arguments for compatibilism and soft determinism. Needless to say, there is the fact that compatibilism would immediately solve the puzzle of how the New Testament could present sin as something which is both inevitable and for which we are responsible: for compatibilism allows that we may be determined to sin and still be free and responsible for it. Furthermore, compatibilism dissolves another puzzle about human freedom: how God could know our future free choices, as well as the counterfactuals of freedom discussed in the previous section. Incompatibilists historically have had some difficulty answering this question, to put it mildly (Vicens and Kittle 2019). Many arguments have also been put forward in support of *theological determinism*, the view that everything – including all human choice – is determined by God. Theists who espouse determinism are generally theological determinists, since the alternative view – that the world is determined, but not by God – would put a serious constraint on divine power. Theological determinists maintain that their view alone respects God's aseity (metaphysical independence), sovereignty, and providential control over the world (Helm 1993; Vicens 2014).

---

[16] See Kane (2005, 24–31) for a discussion of objections to the Consequence Argument, and Demetriou (2010) and McKenna (2008) for objections to the Manipulation Argument.
[17] See Watson (1975), Wolf (1990), Fischer and Ravizza (1998) for alternative compatibilist accounts of free will.

Soft determinists may argue that in addition to the philosophical and theological considerations just mentioned, their view is supported by New Testament portrayals of human freedom. Paul, for instance, seems like a compatibilist at points in his letters. In Romans, for instance, while working out (with "great sorrow and unceasing anguish in [his] heart" – 9:1) how some of his own people could lack faith in Christ, Paul reasons that "not all Israelites truly belong to Israel," and cites as biblical evidence the story of Rebecca and her children:

> Even before they had been born or had done anything good or bad (so that God's purpose of election might continue, not by works but by his call) she was told, "The elder shall serve the younger." As it is written,
> "I have loved Jacob,
>   but I have hated Esau."
> What then are we to say? Is there injustice on God's part? By no means!
> ... For the scripture says to Pharaoh, "I have raised you up for the very purpose of showing my power in you, so that my name may be proclaimed in all the earth." So then he has mercy on whomsoever he chooses, and he hardens the heart of whomsoever he chooses. (Romans 9:11–14, 17–18)

Here Paul seems to accentuate the deterministic nature of God's hardening the heart of Pharoah, who refused to release the people of Israel from slavery and was punished by God for his refusal (see Exodus 9). Thus Paul suggests that Pharoah's being determined to sin is compatible with his responsibility for that sin. Of course, there are other ways to read this Exodus passage; after all, Pharoah hardens his own heart several times before God is said to harden it, so perhaps Pharoah is only responsible for his subsequent sins, which God determines him to commit, because he exercised (libertarian) free will with respect to earlier sin. (See also Stump 1988.) But this does not seem to be the thrust of Paul's thinking more generally in Romans. Later he writes,

> You will say to me then, "Why then does he still find fault? For who can resist his will?" But who indeed are you, a human being, to argue with God? Will what is moulded say to the one who moulds it, "Why have you made me like this?" Has the potter no right over the clay, to make out of the same lump one object for special use and another for ordinary use? What if God, desiring to show his wrath and to make known his power, has endured with much patience the objects of wrath that are made for destruction; and what if he has done so in order to make known the riches of his glory for the objects of mercy, which he has prepared beforehand for glory? (Romans 9:19–24)

The analogy of God and humans to a potter and his clay, and the emphasis on God's preparations "beforehand" and irresistible will, seem categorically deterministic in nature.[18] And yet Paul appears (here, at least[19]) not to find inappropriate God's showing wrath toward those who are "made for destruction."

Other New Testament passages that might be considered to support a compatibilist conception of free will include the following:

> For whoever was called in the Lord as a slave is a freed person belonging to the Lord, just as whoever was free when called is a slave of Christ. (1 Cor. 7:22)

> Now the Lord is the Spirit, and where the Spirit of the Lord is, there is freedom. And all of us, with unveiled faces, seeing the glory of the Lord as though reflected in a mirror, are being transformed into the same image from one degree of glory to another; for this comes from the Lord, the Spirit. (2 Cor. 17–18)

> Present yourselves to God as those who have been brought from death to life, and present your members to God as instruments of righteousness. For sin will have no dominion over you, since you are not under law but under grace. (Romans 6:13–14)

> Thanks be to God that you, having once been slaves of sin, have become obedient from the heart to the form of teaching to which you were entrusted, and that you, having been set free from sin, have become slaves of righteousness. (Romans 6:17–18)

> The law of the Spirit of life in Christ Jesus has set you free from the law of sin and of death. For God has done what the law, weakened by the flesh, could not do: by sending his own Son in the likeness of sinful flesh, and to deal with sin, he condemned sin in the flesh, so that the just requirement of the law might be fulfilled in us, who walk not according to the flesh but according to the Spirit. (Romans 8:2–4)

One natural reading of these passages is that our actions are always determined by something (good or bad desires, say); we are always "slaves" or "obedient" to something – always under the "dominion" of some power or "law." But we are free in the sense required for being responsible for what we do (sin) insofar as we

---

[18] Some biblical scholars find this interpretation less than obvious. Ben Witherington III, for instance, notes that different verbs are used to describe the objects of wrath and mercy: "The vessels of wrath are framed/prepared/fit/put together for wrath while the vessels of mercy are prepared beforehand for glory.... This change in verbs cannot be accidental, and it suggests that Paul means that the vessels of wrath are ripe or fit for destruction. Indeed one could follow the translation of John Chrysostom here and render it ... 'have made themselves fit for' destruction" (2005, 147). Witherington also maintains that the emphasis in this passage is on "God's patience and mercy, giving time for amendment of life" (2005, 146) and notes that other New Testament passages such as Ephesians 2:3–4 make clear that "someone can start out as a vessel of wrath and later become a child of God" (2005, 147).

[19] I will revisit Paul's view in light of other passages from his letters in the next chapter.

do what we want (or, on a more sophisticated compatibilist view, insofar as we have the will we want to have, or act in accord with our deepest values). Then Christ "makes us free" to be "slaves of righteousness," by "condemning sin in the flesh" or "transforming" us through "grace," that is, weakening the hold of our sinful desires on us and strengthening our desires for the good, or God's will; this is what it means to "walk according to the Spirit" or for Christ to live in us.

In sum, soft theological determinism can easily solve the puzzle of sin and free will – how we can be free and responsible for sin that is inevitable. And, as noted in the previous section, compatibilists can make sense of the Augustinian idea that because of the sin of our ancestor(s), all are born into a corrupted state that makes (culpable) sin inevitable for each individual. Furthermore, soft theological determinism can account for the compatibility of freedom and foreknowledge (and counterfactual knowledge); is arguably supported by considerations of divine perfection – God's sovereignty, aseity, and the like; and seems one natural reading of the New Testament portrait of human bondage and freedom.

Divine Causation and Culpability

And yet, according to its critics, theological determinism faces a fatal flaw, in making God "the author" or cause of sin. Some theological determinists vehemently deny this charge, maintaining that since sin is a mere privation of good, God does not cause sin itself. A privative view of sin was suggested by Augustine and developed by Aquinas. According to W. Matthews Grant, Aquinas held that while God, the cause of all being and motion, causes each *act* of sin, sin is "an act with a defect." Thus, "To cause a sin . . . one must cause both the act and the defect. But, while the creature causes both, God does not cause the defect, only the act" (Grant 2009, 456). Grant explains that a person causes the defect in an act of sin by a particular "absence of action" on her part – namely, by her failure to apply "the rule of reason and divine law" to figure out what she ought to do (2009, 462).

One might wonder why *we* count as the cause of the defect of our act in virtue of an absence of action, but God does not; the reason, according to Aquinas (and Grant) is that our absence of action meets certain further conditions that God's does not.[20] The discussion here gets technical rather quickly, and Aquinas's privative view of sin depends on a number of controversial assumptions that have been challenged.[21] Rather than diving into this debate, we may note that the charge that God is the cause of sin is generally taken to be concerning

---

[20] See Grant (2009) for further elaboration.

[21] For a critique of Grant's Thomistic view see Vicens (2012a) and Furlong (2019).

because it introduces the possibility that God could be *culpable* for causing sin. But one may be culpable for what one does not cause. As Heath White notes, "The main motivation for insisting that God causes no evil is undoubtedly to absolve God from responsibility for evil. But then a *non sequitur* threatens. If God creates a piece of Swiss cheese, it may be strictly correct to say that he does not cause the holes in the cheese, but it would defy credulity to say that God is not responsible for the holes in the cheese" (2016, 88). So, we must consider the issue of divine culpability for the sin that, according to soft theological determinism, God determines.

Most theological determinists maintain that even if God is the cause of sin, this does not have unacceptable implications. Hugh McCann, for instance, argues that God's causing sin or moral evil (which McCann seems to equate) does not make God's doing so morally evil (1995) or sinful (2005). For, first, McCann notes, what is predicated of God is quite different than what is predicated of us who sin; we make decisions with evil intentions – to bring down a rival, say, and so to give ourselves a competitive edge – whereas God causes these decisions for entirely different, and much better, purposes (see also Helm 2010, 119). One may think of Joseph saying to his brothers, "Even though you intended to do harm to me, God intended it for good, in order to preserve a numerous people, as he is doing today" (Genesis 50:20). If God has such good intentions, McCann reasons, "then God's goodness is no more impugned by His creating me the person who decides as I do [to sin] than a mother's goodness is impugned by giving her sick child bitter medicine" (1995, 589).

McCann seems right about the first point – God need not have the same intentions as sinners, in causing them to sin – but in offering his analogy of a mother giving a child bitter medicine, he seems to miss a crucial difference: God is not simply causing the evil of *suffering*, in causing people to sin; He is also causing the evil of *sin*! And this seems decidedly worse. We might compare a mother who causes her children to *suffer* for some greater good – their health, say, or longer-term happiness – with a mother who causes her children to *sin* – say, by lying, cheating, and stealing – for similar greater goods. Surely, the latter is worse than the former. And as many authors contend, the biblical narrative presents God as unambiguously *opposed* to sin. Thomas McCall notes that the book of Genesis, along with the rest of Scripture, portrays sin as "the intruder that violates what God has created and called *good*" (2019, 128; see also Rogers 2002, 79), while Thomas Talbott asserts that according to "the Christian understanding," "sin stands in fundamental opposition to God's will for our lives" (2008, 300).[22]

---

[22] In an essay arguing that evolutionary theory problematizes the doctrine of sin, Hans Madueme writes that "Evolution . . . drives a wedge between creation and redemption" since if evolutionary theory is correct, God the Redeemer vanquishes the sin and death that are part of the natural

Theological determinists may reply that on their view, too, sin is in opposition to God's will; for they may distinguish between God's *antecedent* will, or what God values in itself, and God's *consequent* will, or what He judges best, all things considered. They may then affirm that God's antecedent will is opposed to sin. For instance, McCann writes,

> In itself, adultery must surely be displeasing to God, so that the Biblical injunction against it is in accord with his antecedent will. It may be, however, that a better world overall will result if certain adulteries occur. Thomas Paine and Alexander Hamilton were both born of adulterous relationships, and no less a figure than Leonardo da Vinci was illegitimate. Despite their wrongness, the liaisons resulting in these births did take place, hence God's consequent will – that is, what he wills all things considered – must surely have been that they occur. (2009, 426)

A critic might further press that this view is unbiblical: God must be wholeheartedly, or with His consequent will, opposed to sin. But McCann notes that "any account on which God knew in creating the world that it was this world he was creating and not some other, must be an account on which every bit of wrongdoing that ever occurs is in accord with his consequent will" (2009, 426). Consider, for instance, the Molinist position: on this view, God knew that if He created the people who actually exist, and He placed them in the circumstances in which they actually live, they would commit the sins that they in fact commit – and God did this anyway. Of course, if the transworld depravity thesis is true, God could not have created free people and prevented their sinning, whereas on the soft theological determinist view, it would seem God could have. But the theological determinist can maintain that sin is necessary to some greater good *other than* libertarian freedom which God could not secure without sin; so, the views are similar in maintaining that God is antecedently opposed to sin, but consequently wills it for some greater good.

Still, there intuitively seems to be some important difference between God's relation to sin on the theological determinist and libertarian accounts. What could the difference be, that has led some (e.g. Byrne 2008, 200) to conclude, reflecting on Paul's prohibition against doing evil "that good may come" (Romans 3:8),[23] that God on the theological determinist account violates this principle, whereas God on the libertarian account does not? The relevant difference would not seem to be the bare fact that on the first view only, God

---

process that God the Creator has designed (2021, 484). The same point might be made more generally about the theological determinist view: God seems at odds with Himself in opposing something which He has instituted, such that "God's creative and redemptive purposes are set over against each other" (2021, 491).

[23] Alexander Pruss calls this the "deontological principle" (2016, 188).

is *causally* responsible. For, as noted above in reflecting on the privative view of sin, the fact that someone is not causally responsible for something does not entail that she is not morally responsible for it; and similarly, we may note that the fact that someone *is* causally responsible for something does not entail that she is morally responsible for it.

Could the difference be that on the theological determinist view, God *intends* evil, whereas on the libertarian view He does not?[24] Some have tried to maintain this, citing the doctrine of double effect, according to which it is always impermissible to cause evil as a means to one's end (since one's means is a part of one's intent), but it may be permissible to cause evil as an unintended but foreseen consequence, or side effect, of one's intentional action. However, the doctrine of double effect is certainly controversial and may be morally untenable,[25] and it seems inaccurate to say that God, at least on the Molinist view, merely allows and does not intend for sin to occur (Rhoda 2010; Vicens and Kittle 2019, 49–53).

Perhaps, then, lying behind the intuition of a relevant difference is that it would not count as "doing evil" were God to choose to create a world in which He knew people would freely sin *if that were the only way He could create a world with free people*; but it would count as doing evil, were God to choose to create a world and determine people to freely sin, *for some other reason.*[26] However, this claim is controversial too, and there are radically divergent intuitions about whether the soft theological determinist, as opposed to, say, the Molinist, could offer an adequate theodicy for sin.[27]

---

[24] Heath White (2016) has argued that one who affirms that God *determines* everything need not also affirm that God *intends* everything – so this could not be the relevant difference between the theological determinist and libertarian views. However, White's suggested picture of how God might deterministically create the world without intending some aspects of it seems an unattractive one, especially for those who find theological determinism compelling. Peter Furlong has likened the picture to that of a person selecting an item from a vending machine, "intending each of its pros . . . while merely foreseeing each of its cons" and has argued that a more attractive analogy to divine creation is that of an author who does not "merely select a book to write out of the many they can imagine" but instead intends each and every word (2019, 117).

[25] See Vicens (2012a) for an argument to this effect.

[26] Pruss suggests that the relevant difference is that libertarians "can give a story on which God intends a set of initial conditions that in fact lead to sin, but God has a reason for intending these initial conditions that is independent of the fact that they lead to sin" (2016, 191) while theological determinists, at least those who are not also natural determinists, cannot. However, I am not certain that these theological determinists cannot give such a story – and even Pruss says, in conclusion, simply that "the task is much more difficult" for them (2016, 193). And anyway, the point does not apply to theological determinists who are also natural determinists.

[27] Because of limitations of space, this chapter does not consider theodicies for sin, or justifications for why God would create a world in which sin proliferates. For some soft theological deterministic theodicies, see Helm (1993, 206–215); McCann (2005); Couenhoven (2007); Byerly (2017).

While theological determinists sometimes argue that God would not be sinful or (morally) culpable for causing sin, assuming He had a good enough reason for doing so, they also sometimes contend that the charge of sinfulness or culpability cannot stick regardless, since the categories of sin or moral wrong-doing cannot apply to God. McCann, for instance, reasons that it is impossible for God to sin, since "to sin is to set oneself in rebellion against God by flaunting his edict, by knowingly deciding or willing what he has forbidden us to do" – and it is not possible for God to set Himself in rebellion against Himself (2005, 151).[28] McCann thus appeals to a divine command theory of morality, or at least sin, in an attempt to avoid the charge of divine culpability or sinfulness for causing sin.

An important thing to note about McCann's argument is that it appeals to the nature of sin as a violation of God's commandments, rather than to God's nature as essentially good. McCann says that he is wary of the latter sort of appeal since God's having to act in certain ways and not others by a necessity of nature would threaten divine freedom (2005, 152). Thus it would seem to follow from McCann's position not simply that God is not *blameworthy* for some particular action He takes, but that God is not *morally responsible* for any action He takes, since God is not subject to the moral law that His commandments establish. In other words, God is neither morally blameworthy nor morally praiseworthy for any of His deeds; He is beyond morality altogether. Many find this implication of a divine command theory of morality to be reason enough to reject it; for as Peter Furlong notes, "most theists seem to think that God is well behaved, and in fact, that divine behavior is to be taken as a model for human conduct" (2019, 130). Another difficulty facing divine command theories is the familiar Euthyphro problem – that if God's commandments determine the content of morality, then morality is arbitrary, such that what is right might have been wrong and vice versa if God had commanded that it be so. Many find theists find this an unacceptable position, though some have tried to develop divine com-mand theories that avoid the arbitrariness problem.[29]

A further problem with McCann's account is that even if sin does amount to flaunting God's commandments, it may not follow that God is incapable of sin, since McCann's reasoning rests on the dubious premise that "no one can be in moral rebellion against himself," since "no one has moral authority over

---

[28] The criticism of McCann's view that follows is largely taken from Vicens (2012a).

[29] See Robert Adams (1999), especially Ch. 11. McCann only briefly considers the arbitrariness problem in a footnote to his paper, writing in response, "Space does not permit adequate treatment of this problem, but I think it may be argued that God's commands are tied to something else he creates – namely, to the nature of things – and so are not arbitrary" (2005, footnote 13). It is unclear to me what he means here.

himself" (2005, 151). McCann offers a human example in an attempt to establish this point; but of course, if divine command theory is true, then God's commandments must be radically different than human ones – for they must ground morality in a way that human commandments cannot. If by giving commandments God could generate moral obligations for His creatures, it is not clear why He could not also generate them for Himself. At least, McCann's analogy does nothing to illuminate why this would not be possible. Moreover, it would at least *seem* possible for God to generate moral obligations that applied to Himself as well as to creatures, if divine command theory were true. For God could simply decree, for example, that it would henceforth be wrong always and everywhere for *anyone* to tell a lie – in which case, it would be as wrong for God to tell a lie as it would be for creatures. There does not seem to be anything inconsistent about this idea, of God binding Himself, or, as some say, "self-limiting." The idea of divine self-limitation is appealed to in various theological contexts. For instance, some theists argue that God limits His providential control and foreknowledge to make "room" for free creatures. And the biblical concept of *covenant* – of God and His people making promises to each other about their future actions – is also a case of divine self-limitation. Thus it seems at least compatible with McCann's divine command theory that God binds Himself to the moral code that He decrees, such that thereafter any action God might take at variance with that code would be morally wrong.

Divine Blame and Punishment

We have seen that a central issue for soft theological determinists to address is the concern that in determining sin, God becomes the "author" of sin *in some objectionable sense.* Other objections have been raised to the idea that God determines sin, which focus on God's *response* to sin. For, as mentioned already, the New Testament portrays God as condemning sin; while there is "no condemnation for those who are in Christ Jesus" (Romans 8:1), all sinners as deserving of condemnation, wrath, and punishment, and saved only by the unmerited grace of God. But then at least two pressing questions present themselves: First, how could it be *just* for God to blame and punish those He has determined to sin? And second, how could God be *loving* toward those He blames and punishes for something He has determined them to do? The first question may be broken into two further questions, focusing on each party to the blaming relation: How could humans be *deserving* of blame that they are determined by God to commit, and how could God have the *standing* to blame those He has determined to sin? These questions are distinct since one person might lack standing to blame another who is blameworthy for some wrongdoing because, say, the first has committed the same wrongdoing.

The question about desert is in a way quite easy to answer: if compatibilism is true, then humans may be fully morally responsible for their actions even though their actions are determined. Of course, compatibilism faces serious objections for just this reason – that it seems unjust to blame determined agents; there are also questions about whether divine determination of our actions would be more or less of a problem for human responsibility than would natural causal determinism.[30] But we will not focus on the details of those arguments here, in part because the issue of God's standing to blame also calls into question the plausibility of compatibilism, according to at least one thinker. Patrick Todd (2012) begins his reasoning by appealing to the intuition many have, that if God determines us to commit wrongdoing, then God cannot blame us for the wrongdoing we commit. Todd then considers and rules out various possible explanations for *why* it would be inappropriate for God to blame us in this case *besides* the fact that we would not be blameworthy. For instance, one might try to argue that God lacks standing to blame people for the sin He determines them to commit because such blame would be in bad faith, since God's determining people to sin shows that He does not really disapprove of sin. However, as noted earlier, on the assumption that an adequate deterministic theodicy can be constructed, it will follow that God does disapprove of (or antecedently will the nonexistence of) sin, but judges that it contributes to some greater good that makes it worth including in creation. One might instead try to reason that God lacks standing to blame people for the sins He has determined because He is *involved* in those sins; yet Todd argues that such involvement only removes standing to blame when one is at fault, and, again, on the assumption of an adequate theodicy, God will not be at fault for the sin He causes. Todd concludes that the only plausible explanation for God's lacking standing to blame the people He determines to sin is that determined sinners are not blameworthy, and more generally, determinism is incompatible with moral responsibility.[31]

As noted above, Todd's argument begins with the premise that it is inappropriate for God to blame those He has determined to sin. Todd admits to having no argument for this premise but submits that it is "eminently plausible" (2012, 16). Not everyone shares this intuition, of course, and it may be, as Furlong

---

[30] Visala (2021), for instance, notes that theological determinism may seem more threatening to our moral responsibility than natural determinism, since in the theological case there is a "manipulating agent" whereas in the natural case we are subject to only impersonal forces. On the other hand, many theological determinists argue that their view does not undermine human freedom in a way that natural determinism does, given unique features of divine causality which make it "non-competitive" with human agency. See Vicens and Kittle (2019, 33–38) for a discussion and critique of this position.

[31] For a lengthier discussion of Todd's argument with objections and replies, see Vicens and Kittle (2019, 61–65).

suggests, that one's intuitions about this issue are tied up with one's judgment about the plausibility of compatibilism, so that "the strength of the intuition may diminish the less one becomes convinced of incompatibilism or the more one becomes convinced of compatibilism" on independent grounds (2019, 215). Yet, while Todd's argument focuses on God's standing to *blame*, Furlong also notes that the same reasoning should apply to God's standing to *punish* (2019, 214) – and I suspect fewer will have the intuition that there is nothing inappropriate about God's *punishing* people for the sins He determines them to commit, than that there's nothing inappropriate about God's *blaming* them in this case. But many soft theological determinists do defend the appropriateness of divine punishment of sinful creatures – even the eternal punishment of hell. We will return to this issue in the next section, but suffice to say for now that a cost, at least for many people, of the soft theological determinist's solution to the puzzle of sin and free will is that it turns out to be entirely appropriate for God to blame *and* punish people for the sins He determines them to commit.

We turn, then, to the second question: (how) could God be *loving* toward those He blames and punishes for something He has determined them to do? The problem here seems especially acute for soft theological determinists who hold that God will punish some people with eternal damnation. As Katherin Rogers reasons in response to the view of McCann, who defends this possibility, "If you love someone, you desire their good .... But it would be perverse to insist that eternal damnation is the *good* of the creature that love would desire" (2007, 304–305). Furlong (2019, 160–175) develops this line of thinking on the analogy of God to a parent and considers a number of unsatisfactory responses to the problem before settling on four possible responses that he judges, though costly, should not simply be ruled out. First, one might reject the possibility of eternal damnation for any determined creature, and embrace universal salvation. Second, one might reason that "the nature of personal identity requires that specific people suffer in particular ways" (2019, 175) so that it would be impossible for God to create particular people whom He loves and *not* eternally damn them. Third, one might maintain that God can love individuals but sacrifice their (eternal) good for the sake of some other, greater good. Or, fourth, one might reject the conception of divine love under consideration. The first possibility, which I ultimately defend in combination with a denial of full moral responsibility, will be considered in more depth in the next section. But it seems that there is a residual problem for soft theological determinists who maintain humans' full moral responsibility, even if they embrace universalism, as long as they maintain that people *deserve* eternal punishment for the sins that God determines them to commit. For it seems still unloving of God to determine people to do something (or be such a way) that would make them *worthy* of hell.

In any case, the cost of the second possibility is (to my mind) an unintuitive conception of personal identity. The idea is that everything about a person, including the sin that she commits and the eternal damnation that she suffers, is essential to her identity, so that God cannot alter her life story (ante- or post-mortem) if He wants to create *her* at all. While one might have independent reason to endorse such a view – Furlong mentions an account on which "individual people are spacetime worms, made up of temporal parts" (2019, 170) – it would seem ad hoc to adopt this view without independent reason, just to solve the theological determinist's problem of divine punishment. So, the real options for soft theological determinists committed to the possibility of hell who do not already espouse such a view of personal identity appear to be the third and fourth. Both, in a way, appeal to divine mystery: the third suggests that there is some great good unknown to us which can be realized only by God's determining the damnation of some individuals – and which is consistent with divine love – while the fourth invokes God's transcendence over human categories and suggests that the nature of divine love is wholly other than human.

Human Response to Sin

One final objection to the idea that God determines sin is that it leads to a problematic sort of doublemindedness about our own sin, since we are supposed to be *regretful* over our sin – wishing it had never occurred – and yet, on the assumption that God (consequently) willed it for some greater good, we should also be *glad* that we sinned (Byrne 2008, 199–200; Rogers 2011; Vicens 2012a; Furlong 2019, 198–203). The best solution I can think of to such problems is to avoid all thinking about sin from God's perspective, keeping our eyes on the ground, so to speak, and focusing on the commandments God has given us (not to sin). But such a solution would seem to be in tension with the Christian practice of striving, through prayer, study of the Scriptures, and the like, to see the events in one's life from God's perspective, and to value them as God would, in His wisdom and benevolence (Vicens 2012a). As Furlong also notes about a similar response to the problem he discusses, the solution seems at odds with the idea "that human agents should strive for union love with God," since such love "involves the adoption of another's values, cares, concerns, and desires as one's own" (Furlong 2019, 198). On the other hand, perhaps the expectation that we humans should adopt such attitudes is unreasonable. Eleonore Stump has likened the attempt "to maintain as good anything that happens, whatever it is, on the grounds that it is what God wills" to the "Whatever Faction" supporting Mao Tse-tung, and criticized it on a number of fronts. She notes that Job's "comforters," who argue that his suffering must be good because it is willed by God, represent the "Whatever Faction of God" (2008, 345) and that Jesus himself expressed attitudes at odds with God's consequent will, in praying *not my will but yours* be done (Stump 2008, 346). Stump suggests that the appropriate way to align oneself with God's will is with God's *antecedent* will (2008, 346); and while her essay focuses on suffering and not sin, we may add that even on theological determinism, God's antecedent will is opposed to sin.

4 Free Will Skeptical Solutions

We have considered, broadly speaking, two types of responses to the puzzle of sin and free will. First, one might deny that sin is or always has been unavoidable for each of us; at some point each of us makes (or on the Molinist view would make) a libertarianly free choice to sin. Or, second, one might maintain that sin is unavoidable because we are determined to sin – ultimately by something over which we have no control – and yet the choice to sin is still free, and something for which we are responsible. In this section we consider the final alternative: not denying the unavoidability of sin or maintaining the compatibility of this unavoidability with free will and moral responsibility, but denying that the choice to sin is (or was) for each of us a free and responsible one.

Denying the Universality of Culpable Sin

There seem as many reasons for denying free will and moral responsibility with respect to sin as there are variations on interpreting exactly what such a denial amounts to. Some do not go so far as to deny any moral responsibility for sin at all, but simply maintain that sin is a larger category than that for which we are morally responsible. For instance, Terence Cuneo maintains that the common (western) conception of sin as "a derelict moral condition" is "extraordinarily pinched" and at odds with the eastern Christian tradition's much broader conception of sin as "a state of deep disorder, which has moral, legal, aesthetic, and therapeutic dimensions," some of which "needn't imply that an agent who suffers from them is morally guilty in virtue of suffering them" (2016, 189). Cuneo asserts that the counterpart to sin is not innocence or goodness, but holiness, which, when ascribed to God, involves the transcendence of "all blemish, taint, disorder, and defilement" (2016, 190). He also suggests a contrast between sin and health, and an association of "the sin-disorder" with sickness (2016, 191). In commenting on the work of the Orthodox theologian Alexander Schmemann, Cuneo writes, "Schmemann suggests that . . . the falling away is the manifestation of an eating disorder" in the form of a loss of hunger for God (2016, 192). He goes on to discuss many parallels between sin and anorexia: those who have these disorders "suffer from a baffling confluence of self-destructive behavior, loss of personal autonomy, and ruthless self-loathing, laced with tendencies to isolate oneself from others, engage in deceptive behavior, and radically misperceive one's own state" (2016, 193); finally, "in both cases, we find ourselves describing the disorders in active terms, as powers to whose influence we do not choose to submit ourselves, but in some sense find ourselves under" (2016, 194). Such a characterization may raise questions for those who understand sin as, by definition, moral wrongdoing against God – say, a violation of divine law or rebellious breach of the divine–human relationship:[32] What does "sin" mean, otherwise? Is there a broader definition that might encompass both western and eastern conceptions of sin? What the different conceptions have in common is that sin is – to borrow the words of Cornelius Plantinga Jr. – "not the way it's supposed to be" (1999). I suggest that we think of sin as something about a person – something *personal* – that is in some sense against God's will, and that harms the divine–human relationship.

It is unclear how to categorize such an understanding of sin in light of the possible responses to the puzzle of sin and free will we have considered. Cuneo does not say that we are *never* morally culpable for sin, or that sin is a completely amoral concept – rather, he says it has both moral and non-moral "dimensions." This suggests that some sin is morally culpable, and other sin is not.[33] We can then ask: Is *culpable* sin universal – that is, is every person (apart from Christ) morally culpable for some sin? If so, then we can home in on culpable sin, and our options for resolving the puzzle will be the two considered already: libertarian and soft determinist. So here I focus on the possibility that while sin is universal, culpable sin is not: some sinners do not (ever) sin culpably.

How would this idea, that all sin, but not all sin culpably, cohere with the biblical data about sin that we considered in Section 1? We would seem to need a two-pronged interpretative strategy. On the one hand, since (not necessarily culpable) sin is universal and unavoidable, salvation from such sin is also a universal need. On the other hand, if culpable sin is not universal, and if divine wrath is deserved only by culpable sinners, then universal salvation cannot be from the wrath of God, and our Savior cannot be one who rescues all sinners from divine wrath. Nor can all sinners be deserving of condemnation.

---

[32] Cornelius Plantinga, Jr., for instance, defines sin as "agential evil for which some person (or group of persons) is to blame. In short, sin is culpable shalom-breaking" (1995, 14).

[33] See also Vicens (2018) for the suggestion that sin is a larger category than that for which we are morally responsible.

Similarly, the injunction to repent of sins, if this is taken to require free will, cannot be directed at all sinners, since some do not have free will with respect to their sins; and forgiveness, if this assumes the responsibility of the forgiven, cannot be granted to all sinners, either.[34] Still, one need not dispense with the concepts of human repentance or divine condemnation, wrath, and forgiveness altogether, for since the view under consideration allows that some sin is culpable, it will follow that some sinners are liable to divine wrath and condemnation, in need of divine forgiveness, and able to respond to an injunction to repent. The point is simply that these things will not universally apply.

Such an implication might seem too high a price to pay for a solution to the puzzle. But it should be noted that something like this view may be represented in the early Christian tradition and in contemporary Orthodox theology. (I say "may," since the ideas I will discuss here are open to another interpretation, discussed at the end of this section along the lines of what I call "sort-of compatibilism.") The Orthodox interpret the story of Adam's sin as the story of every person "rather than, or at least as much as" a historical account (Louth 2013, 72); and according to the Orthodox scholar Andrew Louth, "Adam unleashed consequences of sin that are more than he could be regarded as personally responsible for" (2013, 72). The Orthodox conception of "ancestral" or inherited sin does not involve the notion of original guilt; as Louth explains, "It is not claimed that we are *responsible* for ancestral sin, simply that we are affected by it" (2013, 78). According to Louth, "the Fathers" held that the main consequence of Adam's disobedience is death, rather than sin: we are (through no fault of our own) born into a world "characterized by corruption, disintegration ... a world in which it is impossible to achieve anything, where all human intentions are like building on sand – they are impermanent, fragile" (2013, 71). Louth suggests that "it is not so much sin that causes death, as death that causes sin" (2013, 71); and "the consequences of sin are amplified, in the course of nature" to be "so much more than [we] could really be blamed for" (2013, 72).

On such a picture, God would approach (at least non-culpable) sin not in wrath, but in compassion. On the view of St. Silouan, an Eastern Orthodox monk, "the story of Adam is ... the story of love lost" by man (Louth 2013, 80); and since lost love is "the main consequence of Adam's sin ... it is the restoration of that love that God seeks from then on. The expulsion from paradise, the nakedness, the toil needed to support themselves, even the pain of childbirth, are seen as ways in which God seeks to stir man's conscience and

---

[34] Later in this section we will consider interpretations of biblical passages about repentance and divine condemnation, wrath, and punishment consistent with a lack of human freedom. Here it is assumed that these passages require free will.

bring him back to love" (2013, 81). Thus what we might think of as retributive punishment is actually rehabilitative. But what about eternal punishment? Louth notes that in contrast to what is found in western theology, "in Orthodox theology hope in universal salvation ... has never gone away .... The grounds for this are principally the long-suffering love of God for all creation, and also the conviction that evil is without substance, but is rather a corruption or distortion of what is good" (2013, 158).[35] The hope, then, is that even for culpable sinners, hell is not a state of eternal retributive punishment – not retributive, because, in the words of Diodore of Tarsus, it is the experience of "the scourge of love" (quoted in Louth 2013, 158), and not eternal, for if sin cannot last forever, neither can hell.

The idea that sin is not fundamentally or essentially something for which we are morally responsible can make sense of the problem, briefly mentioned in Section 2, of how even infants and young children can be sinners. This problem becomes acute when thinking about those who die very young, raising the question of whether they are in need of salvation from sin. While the problem was presented in a discussion of libertarianism, it seems just as acute for soft determinists who affirm that all are culpable sinners; for, surely, those who die in infancy lack the capacities for moral responsibility. Section 2 considered one proposed solution to this problem – Mark Anderson's suggestion to look to counterfactual sin: these little ones *would* (culpably) sin, were they mature agents in certain circumstances. While the proposal was offered on behalf of the Molinist, it seems compatible with soft determinism as well. But a number of difficulties with this proposal have been noted; and it is also not clear how it would apply to those who, due to a severe disability, *never* develop the capacities requisite for moral responsibility. What, after all, is the "naked will" of those who lack these capacities, which could be put upon the "scales of justice"? The Augustinian realist account of original sin that some libertarians appeal to may likewise seem puzzling when applied to those who die in infancy: How could they have participated in and so be morally responsible for Adam's sin? On the approach under consideration here, in contrast, we need not attribute culpable sin to apparently innocent children or adults who lack the capacities for moral responsibility. Rather, we need only note that they are born into a fallen, broken world where they are influenced by forces over which they have no control, and which produce unhealthy behaviors whose consequences they cannot be blamed for.[36]

---

[35] Interestingly, while western theologians following St. Augustine take the privative nature of evil to mean that God is not the author of sin, at least some eastern Christians take it to mean that sin cannot exist in the eternal presence of God!

[36] Crisp proposes a similar view of infant sin in (2020); however, on his view, all people who do not die in infancy or have a severe mental incapacity become responsible for committing sin that

The most significant cost to the view sketched here is that it leads to a problematic bifurcation among sinners. Recall that we are assuming, for the sake of argument, that some but not all sinners are culpable – for, again, if all are culpable sinners, then we may return to the libertarian or soft determinist interpretations of how this could be so. And if some but not all sinners are culpable, then this means that *some but not all sinners are deserving of divine condemnation, wrath, and punishment* – even before any are saved. But, setting aside the issue of the very young and cognitively disabled who seem to lack moral responsibility and focusing solely on cognitively able adults, the New Testament does not present such a bifurcated view of sinners. When Paul says that "one man's trespass led to condemnation for all" (Romans 5:18), he seems to really mean *all*. And when he describes Jesus as the one "who rescues us from the wrath that is coming" (1 Thess. 1:10), it strains credulity to believe that only some are subject to "the wrath" even without the rescuing of Jesus. So, if we are going to deny that sin is fundamentally or essentially something for which we are morally responsible, we should try to avoid the bifurcated view on which some but not all (mature, cognitively able) sinners are culpable for their sin.[37] Thus we next turn to the possibility that *no* sinners are culpable for their sin, because no sinners are free or morally responsible.

Introducing "Basic-desert" Moral Responsibility Skepticism

As with libertarianism and soft determinism, a wide variety of reasons has been offered for free will and moral responsibility skepticism. One might argue first that free will and determinism are incompatible, along the lines considered in Section 2 (e.g. the Consequence Argument or the Manipulation Argument), and then that we do not have good evidence that determinism is false, or that we have some reason to think, at the microphysical or biological or psychological level, that determinism is true (see Caruso 2012). Or one might combine an argument for incompatibilism with theological reasoning in support of deter- minism, along the lines suggested in Section 3 (e.g. considerations of divine aseity, sovereignty, providential control, or foreknowledge). Of course, the puzzle of sin and free will might itself lead to skepticism, if one finds the resolutions to the puzzle discussed in the previous two secions untenable. It should be noted that one need not be a determinist, or even have suspicions that

---

their corrupted condition "*normally inevitably yields*" (2020, 45) – whereas on the view under consideration, some competent adults still do not commit culpable sin.

[37] I'm not even sure that this view makes much sense with applied to infants. I suggested above that one might say that infants are sinners in the sense that they behave in unhealthy ways. But, as I suggested above, sin seems fundamentally something *personal*, or, as I will later put the point, *attributable* to a person's deep self; and infants don't (yet) have a deep self.

determinism is true, to be a skeptic. One might be a "hard incompatibilist," thinking that if free will is not compatible with determinism, neither is it compatible with indeterminism – for indeterminism simply introduces randomness into one's actions and does not provide a locus of control (Levy 2011). One might maintain that such control is at least metaphysically possible, in the form of an agent causing her action for herself rather than being determined by various antecedent events – but then contend that there is no evidence that we have (or some evidence that we lack) such "agent-causal" control (Pereboom 2014). Of course, if one is a free will skeptic but denies that human choices are (presently) determined, then one's skepticism will not help in accounting for the unavoidability of sin. For this reason, I focus here on the view that we lack free will *and* (perhaps *because*) our choices are determined. Finally, one might be a free will skeptic, in the sense that I mean, without denying that human beings *ever* had free will, or that their choices were *always* determined. For one might be skeptical that we humans today lack free will, for instance, on the grounds of the inevitability of sin, but allow that earlier humans had free will, say, before the fall of Adam. We will return to this possibility shortly.

On the assumption that free will is required for moral responsibility, free will skepticism immediately leads to moral responsibility skepticism. But moral responsibility seems assumed by the attitudes that many take to be essential to the most valuable human relationships – attitudes such as gratitude, love, forgiveness, anger, guilt, and remorse. P. F. Strawson famously argued that without such "reactive" attitudes – attitudes, that is, that are reactions to the good or ill will of others (or ourselves), we are left only with an "objective" attitude – a perspective on which others are things "to be managed or handled or cured or trained" (1963, 79). Strawson maintained that "A sustained objectivity of inter-personal attitude, and the human isolation which that would entail, does not seem to be something of which human beings would be capable, even if some general truth were a theoretical ground for it" (1963, 81); and even if we could maintain such an attitude toward others (and ourselves), our lives and relationships would surely be very much impoverished by it. Thus many, with Strawson, have concluded that free will skepticism is unacceptable, being incompatible with a meaningful and fulfilling human life.

In response, some free will skeptics have argued that the implications of free will skepticism are not as bad as they seem. In what follows, I concentrate on the reasoning of Derk Pereboom, whose defense of free will skepticism is the most extensive in recent philosophical literature. First, Pereboom notes that free will skepticism does not rule out all attitudes and practices associated with holding responsible. Instead, it rules out only the assumption of "basic desert," i.e. that people deserve responses of praise and blame, reward and punishment simply in virtue of the moral status of their actions (2014, 2). But we might praise or blame, reward or punish someone for reasons other than basic desert. For instance, a child might be disciplined by her parents or teachers so that she behaves better in the future, or because she has broken a rule. The first reason is a *consequentialist* or *forward-looking* reason: she is disciplined for the good that it will do; the second is *contractualist*, appealing to the violation of an agreed-upon rule. While in the latter case, we might say that the child *deserves* discipline, our justification for saying this will appeal in part to the rule she has broken. In contrast, a basic-desert justification would appeal only to the moral status of her action.

This appeal to the common way we treat children might invoke Strawson's concern about the objective attitude, however; for we often treat children, especially young ones who are not ("basic-desert") morally responsible for their behavior, as subjects to be "managed or handled or cured or trained." But Pereboom argues that the attitudes that are most important to meaningful relationships between adults are not threatened by his moral responsibility skepticism. For instance, he reasons, "Gratitude involves . . . being thankful toward someone who has acted beneficially" and while this may often involve the belief that the benefactor has basic-desert moral responsibility, it need not (2014, 190). Similarly, much valuable human love is neither freely chosen by the lover, nor basically deserved by the beloved. On the first count, Pereboom points to romantic love as an attitude that the lovers often simply find themselves experiencing, without any movement of the will, much less *free* will. On the second point, he similarly notes that adults often love each other for reasons that have nothing to do with basic desert. Pereboom concludes, "Love of another involves, most fundamentally, wishing well for the other, taking on aims and projects of the other as one's own, and a desire to be together with the other. Free will skepticism does not threaten any of this" (2014, 190).

While Pereboom defends the compatibility of such positive attitudes with basic-desert moral responsibility skepticism, he takes a different approach when it comes to negative attitudes such as anger and resentment, arguing that if they are incompatible with such skepticism, we would be better off without them. For anger and related emotions have significant negative effects. For instance, "expression of anger tends to allow only either a humiliating or else a defiant response" and "when people are angry . . . they tend to misrepresent relevant features of the situation"; both of these effects hinder reform and reconciliation (2021, 3). And there is anthropological evidence that humans are malleable enough to significantly reduce expressions of anger under the right conditions (2021, 6). Finally, Pereboom appeals to the teachings of Christianity, as well as other world religions and philosophies such as Buddhism and Stoicism, which discourage human anger, and he instead recommends practices of holding responsible on forward-looking grounds (2021, 6).[38]

As we noted in Secion 1, forgiveness is normally distinguished from excuse on the basis of responsibility ascriptions: you may be excused if it turns out you were not responsible for wronging someone, while you would only seem to be forgivable if you were responsible for wrongdoing. Moreover, forgiveness is often characterized as the overcoming or foreswearing of resentment or similar negative reactive attitudes. How, then, can a free will skeptic allow for the possibility of forgiveness? Pereboom begins with an account of blame as moral protest – "a stance of opposition to an agent" for engaging in wrongdoing, with the function of communicating one's opposition and the reasons for one's opposition (2021, 39–40). He notes that one might protest wrongdoing without any assumption that the wrongdoer is basic-desert morally responsible for what she has done (2021, 40). He then proposes an account of forgiveness as the renunciation of moral protest; and following Pamela Hieronymi, he suggests that such a renunciation is normally appropriate if and only if the wrongdoer has expressed a recognition of the unacceptability of what she has done (2021, 109–111).

Finally, regarding so-called self-reactive attitudes such as guilt and remorse, Pereboom argues that while the assumption of basic desert is incompatible with his view, he can still maintain self-blaming attitudes similar to those involved in the protest of others. He writes, "One might view an action one has performed as wrong, and the disposition that issues in it as morally defective, and as a result take on a stance of opposition against oneself for having performed the action.... In adopting this stance, one may aim at one's own moral formation or at reconciliation with someone one has wronged" (2021, 48). Thus Pereboom invokes forward-looking justifications for these reactive attitudes. And he implies that Strawson has presented us with a false dilemma in arguing that the rejection of basic desert and the assumption of consequentialist justifications for practices of holding responsible would require us to adopt objective attitudes toward each other. Pereboom shows that the most important attitudes we take toward each other are not undermined by the rejection of basic desert, and that meaningful lives and relationships may be retained.

---

[38] See also Talbott, who argues that "Jesus and Paul consistently rejected as inappropriate the very reactive attitudes upon which so many rest their understanding of moral guilt" (2008, 306).

Divine Condemnation, Wrath, and Punishment

How does basic-desert moral responsibility skepticism measure up, theologically? The skeptic would not seem able to take literally the many biblical references to divine anger or wrath, since such reactive attitudes assume the basic-desert moral responsibility of their targets. Nor is divine condemnation appropriate on this view, since condemnation involves a judgment of guilt. Finally, the skeptic must reject any form of retributive punishment, including, presumably, hell. And while free will believers may have grounds for hope that God's mercy will lead to universal salvation, for the skeptic this is a matter not of mercy, but of justice: any divine wrath, condemnation, and retributive punishment would be *wrong*, since none deserve it.

This may seem like a lot to give up, since, as noted in Secion 1, the New Testament is replete with the language of divine judgment, condemnation, wrath, and (apparently retributive) punishment. But the basic-desert moral responsibility skeptic may offer alternative interpretations of these biblical concepts and argue that such alternatives better fit with the overall picture of human sin presented in the New Testament. Below I do my best, on behalf of Pereboom, to sketch a biblical interpretation consistent with basic-desert moral responsibility skepticism, before going on to raise some objections to it.

On Pereboom's view, it should be remembered that blame is possible even in the absence of basic-desert moral responsibility skepticism. While Pereboom exclusively discusses *human* blame, his view would also seem to allow the possibility of divine blame, expressed for God's own forward-looking purposes. And while he argues that anger involves unwarranted assumptions and has frequent negative effects, perhaps he could interpret divine wrath as different in nature than human anger. For instance, human anger is directed at *persons* and tends to involve the assumption that its targets are (basic-desert) morally responsible for their wrongdoing. In contrast, according to the biblical scholar Christopher Marshall, in the New Testament the target of wrath is not the person who sins, but the sin which overpowers the sinner. In analyzing the view of Paul, Marshall argues that *sin* "designates God's fervent reaction against human wickedness, God's refusal to tolerate, compromise with, or indulge evil .... Wrath is ... a measured commitment to act against evil and injustice in order to contain and destroy it" (2001, 171). Marshall concludes that "the cross supremely reveals God's wrath not because sinners are vicariously punished in the experience of Christ but because the cross definitively subverts and destroys the principle of sin itself" (2001, 173).[39]

As for punishment, Marshall suggests that Paul's recommendations for those within the church – which "range from admonition to rebuke to temporary expulsion" (2001, 149) – serve to "protect the community from contamination with evil, and to encourage repentance and restoration of the obstinate sinner" (2001, 155), while his frequent use of curses functions to "reinforce the moral . . . boundaries of a community" by identifying "certain kinds of behavior as especially offensive or dangerous" (2001, 166). None of this suggests a retributive view of punishment, at least in the human sphere. And regarding divine punishment, Thomas Talbott likewise argues that the ideas of "intrinsic desert" and "metaphysical guilt" played no substantial role in the thinking of either Jesus or Paul; in response to the question of what it could then mean to say that certain sins are "worthy of death" (Romans 1:32; the NRSV says that certain people "deserve to die"), Talbott reasons that *death* refers to "separation from God and from the ultimate source of human happiness," which is what one chooses in sinning. Thus, Talbott concludes, "death, which is the unavoidable consequence of sin, is itself intrinsically fitting punishment only in the sense that a painful burn is the intrinsically fitting punishment for intentionally thrusting one's hand into a fire" (2008, 306). In other words, death is not really a punishment for sin at all, much less a retributive punishment.

Finally, when it comes to the ultimate retributive divine punishment – hell – we have already seen within historical Christianity a tradition of hope for universal salvation. A number of philosophers have more recently offered arguments supporting universalism, from biblical texts emphasizing the universal scope of God's love, mercy, and salvation to theological considerations of God's justice, goodness, power, and effectiveness in bringing about His purposes. Pereboom, for instance, maintains that the "most reasonable reading of the texts of Christian scriptures might well be on the side of universalism," while Talbott contends "that the universalism of the New Testament is not only pervasive, but clear and obvious as well" (1999, 55). Both cite, among other passages, Romans 5:18 ("just as one man's trespass led to condemnation for all, so one man's act of righteousness leads to justification and life for all") and Colossians 1:20 ("through him God was pleased to reconcile to himself all things, whether on earth or in heaven, by making peace through the blood of his cross") (Talbott 1999, 56 and 66; Pereboom 2016, 119 and footnote 28). As for what to do with the many apparent references to eternal punishment and the like

---

[39] Aku Visala has suggested (in personal communication) that Luther also might have held that divine wrath is not deserved by sinners but rather expressed so that "they might turn to God and be saved."

in Scripture, Talbott maintains that they are misinterpreted. For instance, he argues that "eternal" does not literally mean *everlasting*, but rather "having its causal source in the eternal God" and "associated with the age to come" (1999, 89, 90), while the word translated "punishment" originally referred to "the pruning of trees to make them grow better" and so should be understood as *remedial* (1999, 91). Putting this altogether, Talbott concludes, "it is, if you will, *an eternal means of correction*. It is eternal both in the sense that its causal source lies in the eternal God himself and in the sense that its corrective effects last forever" (1999, 91). Other interpreters suggest that biblical references to hell may be metaphorical. Marilyn McCord Adams, for instance, proposes that they express the "deep truth" of "how *bad* it is, how utterly indecent, not to respond to God appropriately" (1993, 324), while Marshall argues that they are intended to convey that "earthly actions have eschatological significance and will receive appropriate recognition from God" (2001, 189).

The Biblical View of Bondage and Freedom

Basic-desert moral responsibility skeptics may argue not only that they have the resources to interpret biblical texts which might seem to support the reality of basic desert, but that their view fits best overall with the biblical picture of human sin and free will. Recall, first, an early Christian interpretation of the story of the fall: as Talbott reports it, the first sinners' sin "was no more a perfectly free choice ... than the disobedient choices of a typical two year old are perfectly free" since it was committed largely in ignorance of good and evil (2008, 310); likewise, Talbott reasons, citing Paul,

> "As was the man of dust, so are those who are of the dust," and this at least suggests that Adam and his descendants ("those who are of the dust") all come into being in the same context of ambiguity, ignorance, and misperception and with similar dispositions and propensities. The Psalmist thus declared that the Lord "does not deal with us according to our sins, nor repay us according to our iniquities." Why not? Because "he knows how we were made; he remembers that we are dust." (2008, 311)

Talbott argues that, like the original sin of Adam and Eve, so our sins – even the worst of them – are, according to the Christian Scriptures, committed in ignorance (2008, footnote 34).

And whether we assume a compatibilist or incompatibilist account of free will, certain New Testament texts suggest that we lack free will with respect to sin. Consider, for instance, the passage in which Paul says, apparently speaking as "every person" before conversion, "I can will what is right, but I cannot do it. For I do not do the good I want, but the evil I do not want is what I do"

(Romans 7:18–19). On Frankfurt's hierarchical account (1971), we might interpret Paul as saying that he has a second-order desire to do the good he wants to do, while his first-order desire to do evil wins out. In this case, Paul would not count as morally responsible for doing evil. Similarly, when he writes, a few verses later, that he is "captive" to the law of sin, in need of "rescue from this body of death" (Romans 7:23–24), we may note that captives in need of rescue are not normally understood to be free and responsible for their state.

Furthermore, while the previous section put forward an interpretation of several biblical passages that seemed amenable to an interpretation on which we are (basic-desert) morally responsible for our sins, these passages seem largely open to an opposing interpretation. Consider them again:

> For whoever was called in the Lord as a slave is a freed person belonging to the Lord, just as whoever was free when called is a slave of Christ. (1 Cor. 7:22)

> Now the Lord is the Spirit, and where the Spirit of the Lord is, there is freedom. And all of us, with unveiled faces, seeing the glory of the Lord as though reflected in a mirror, are being transformed into the same image from one degree of glory to another; for this comes from the Lord, the Spirit. (2 Cor. 17–18)

> Present yourselves to God as those who have been brought from death to life, and present your members to God as instruments of righteousness. For sin will have no dominion over you, since you are not under law but under grace. (Romans 6:13–14)

> Thanks be to God that you, having once been slaves of sin, have become obedient from the heart to the form of teaching to which you were entrusted, and that you, having been set free from sin, have become slaves of righteousness. (Romans 6:17–18)

> The law of the Spirit of life in Christ Jesus has set you free from the law of sin and of death. For God has done what the law, weakened by the flesh, could not do: by sending his own Son in the likeness of sinful flesh, and to deal with sin, he condemned sin in the flesh, so that the just requirement of the law might be fulfilled in us, who walk not according to the flesh but according to the Spirit. (Romans 8:2–4)

Previously, I suggested that these passages are consistent with a theory of freedom on which we are always determined by something – good or bad desires, say – and that our conversion amounts to God's weakening the hold of our sinful desires on us and strengthening our desires for the good. On such a view, we would be free and responsible, whether we are "slaves of sin" or "slaves of righteousness." Other than the first passage, however, none indicates that we are free *before* being touched by God's grace. And, indeed, several suggest the opposite: that we only gain freedom after being "called" or "transformed" or, more dramatically, "brought from death to life." While Pereboom doesn't focus on the possibility of our gaining free will and thus becoming basic-desert morally responsible, this possibility seems compatible with his view.

Repentance

Another issue facing basic-desert moral responsibility skepticism is its ability to account for human repentance. As discussed in Section 1, people are commanded by Jesus and his followers to repent of sin; but this commandment seems to imply that people are responsible for sin. Timothy O'Connor has elaborated on the idea that true repentance is not possible, if basic-desert moral responsibility skepticism is true. True repentance, he maintains, involves not only an acknowledgment of one's sinfulness and expressed desire to change, but also "a sincere pledge to do what is required of us and acceptance that we are accountable for our following through or not" (2016, 138). O'Connor muses that without such a pledge and acceptance, confession and repentance might sound like this:

> Yes, God, I agree, that what you have made of me thus far is flawed in respects X, Y, and Z. I don't like that any more than you do (or, than you do in your "revealed," if not "secret" will, or some such thing). I'm on board with changing those things straightaway. I'll do my part, if that is what you have foreordained me to do. If not, not. You're calling the shots. If I blow it again, then I'll confess it again and see what you have in mind the next go-round. Since I am confessing, I confess this all leaves me a bit confused. I'm not making excuses, exactly (although I am blameless). These features really do stink, and they ought to change. Here's hoping they do. (2016, 138)

This certainly seems like an unacceptable form of repentance! But the problem might be exaggerated; after all, in many cases of genuine repentance we don't expect the repentant to have confidence that she will not fall back into her old ways, or a sense of responsibility for these old ways. Consider, for instance, someone struggling with drug or alcohol addiction, who acknowledges her moral failings – the bad choices she has made, the way her choices have harmed her loved ones and herself – and expresses a sincere desire to change; and suppose she is taking steps (joining a support group, entering rehab, etc.) to make these changes permanent. Of course, she may have gone down this path before, only to relapse, so she should acknowledge the possibility of this happening again. And she may believe that the causal factors influencing her previous relapses undermined her "basic desert" responsibility for her failures. And yet, genuine repentance may still take place. What makes this genuine repentance is not any confidence of her ability to make this change permanent, nor confidence that God will ensure her permanent reform; it is, instead, the act of *turning* itself – in this case, turning away from a way of life governed by her desires for drugs, and to a life devoted to something else – her family, perhaps, or God. And this turning is surely compatible with skepticism about her control over and responsibility for her past or future behavior.

Moreover, it bears repeating that skepticism about our basic-desert moral responsibility for sin does not necessarily commit one to skepticism about any human moral responsibility, ever. One might maintain instead that, as slaves of sin, we are unfree *until* God sets us free. If repentance takes place after, or in the midst of, God's granting us freedom, then it would seem O'Connor's criticisms need not apply; for then we could offer a sincere pledge to do what is required of us, and accept that we are accountable for our following through or not.

Divine Authorship of Sin

For those who are skeptical of basic-desert moral responsibility on the grounds that determinism and incompatibilism are both true ("hard determinists") the issue of God's authorship of sin would seem to be similar to that facing soft determinists. However, Pereboom contends that the problem of divine authorship of sin is not as difficult on hard determinism as on soft, for although God must be said to cause sin in either case, on the former view He is not the cause of *culpable* sin. Thus the concern that our culpability could somehow transfer to the One who determined us to sin is alleviated. Pereboom reasons that on his view, "God's causing our immoral intentions and actions is more similar to causing natural evils, such as earthquakes and diseases, than it is on a view according to which we are blameworthy in the basic desert sense. As a result, the concern that God is the author of sin is closer to a problem that all traditional theists face, i.e. how God can cause ... natural evil" (2016, 116; see also Helm 1993, 198).

Of course, the basic-desert moral responsibility skeptic is not out of the woods yet, for it is no small thing to account for God's allowing even natural evils – and, as Pereboom notes, "as God's power over evil is increased [as it is on theological determinism], God's policies become more mysterious, given the amount of evil in the world" (2016, 128). Still, a number of explanations for evil in a deterministic world have been proposed, including those that appeal to the good of natural laws, evolution, or human development. For instance, Pereboom contends, commenting on John Hick's soul-making theodicy:

The process of educating and developing our characters, sensitivities, and abilities, even conceived without the freedom required for moral responsibility in the basic desert sense, is a great good. Arguably, the development from cowardice to courage, from immorality to morality, from ignorance to enlightenment, is valuable, even if these processes are wholly causally determined by God in such a way as to exclude moral responsibility in this sense. (2016, 125)

Other theodicies that might be amenable to moral responsibility skepticism include those that appeal to the good of divine forgiveness (Helm 1993, 213–215), human conversion (Stump 1985), or human identification with God (Adams 1999). The moral responsibility skeptic might also deny the need for a theodicy for sin, arguing that humans should not be expected to understand God's reasons for creating and governing the world as He does. This is a position known as "skeptical theism" (see McBrayer 2010).

In the previous section, we raised two questions for the soft theological determinist, regarding God's response to human sin: How could it be *just* for God to blame and punish those He has determined to sin, and how could God be *loving* toward those He blames and punishes for something He has determined them to do? The same questions may be asked of the hard theological determinist. Like the issue of divine authorship of and culpability for causing sin, the question about divine love in blaming and punishing sinners might actually be easier for the hard determinist to answer than for the soft. After all, divine blame, and punishment, on a view like Pereboom's, has forward-looking justifications, such as that these divine responses to sin facilitate moral reform and reconciliation; and love seems more congruent with these aims than with retributive punishment, especially of the eternal sort. (We are assuming here that the basic-desert moral responsibility skeptic is committed to universalism.) Regarding the justice question, the critic may note that, according to the basic-desert moral responsibility skeptic, sinners are not *deserving* of blame or punishment – so how could it be fair to blame or punish them? But the skeptic may respond by pointing out that it is sometimes just to treat people in (negative) ways, even if they do not ("basically") deserve this treatment. For instance, it is just for me to take Monopoly money from you if you land on my property in the game; more seriously, it is (arguably) just for the government to quarantine someone with a deadly contagious disease such as Ebola.[40]

For those especially troubled by a determining God's responsibility for and response to human sin, it should be noted that skepticism about human moral responsibility – even on the grounds that our sin is now determined by forces

---

[40] In fact, Pereboom has proposed a quarantine model of punishment for those who lack basic-desert moral responsibility but are a danger to others (2014, 169–173).

beyond our control, for which we are not responsible – does not by itself entail determinism. One might maintain instead that humans originally had (libertarian) free will, but, having misused it, have since become "slaves of sin" (Romans 6:20). According to Lynne Rudder Baker, Augustine may have held that "Adam had free will as libertarians construe it, but the Fall destroyed it for Adam and his descendants" (2003, 463); this may have been Luther's view as well. Yet Augustine (and Luther) certainly maintained that postlapsarian humans were (basic-desert) morally responsible for their sin, and thus they seemed to have been compatibilists.[41] The view under consideration here, instead, is an incompatibilist one: since present-day humans are determined to sin through no fault of their own, they are not culpable sinners. Such a view may seem to involve the worst of both worlds, so to speak: the inability to claim the benefits of theological determinism, such as a strong doctrine of divine sovereignty and providential control over creation, *and* the inability to affirm present-day human moral responsibility. And yet, some have found it a step up from hard determinism, on the grounds that, as Timothy O'Connor puts it, "It seems easier to accept such a world as consistent with God's perfect goodness than a world where He directly wills acts of grave moral evil" (2016, 137). Talbott similarly reasons, "Whether or not a Christian can consistently be a compatibilist, consistently be a libertarian, or even consistently hold that the concepts of *freewill* and *moral responsibility* are ultimately incoherent, the Christian understanding of sin – the idea that sin stands in fundamental opposition to God's will for our lives – is nonetheless incompatible with a thorough going determinism" (2008, 300). Different thinkers will weigh the costs and benefits of such options differently.[42]

Critique and Proposal: Basic-Desert Moral Responsibility without Retributivism

While Pereboom doubts the reality of "basic-desert" moral responsibility, he maintains the existence of other forms or "senses" of responsibility, which are differentiated according to their aims and justifications (2017, 121–122). As indicated already, the form that he focuses on is justified by its "forward-looking" aims. One might argue, however, that the concept of moral responsibility cannot be divorced from basic desert; and to say that we are justified, for instance, in protesting someone's behavior based on the forward-looking

---

[41] Strictly speaking, Luther should be categorized as a "semi-compatibilist": one who thinks that moral responsibility *but not free will* is compatible with determinism. See Visala and Vainio (2020).

[42] Following Vicens (2022b), I remain agnostic on the question of how to weigh these costs and benefits.

consideration that protest would likely achieve certain goods isn't to say that the target of our protest is in *any* sense morally responsible. Whether we call it a form of moral responsibility or not, though, Pereboom's substantial claim is that the attitudes and practices we normally associate with moral responsibility, and that he thinks are worth retaining – such as blame-as-protest and forgiveness-as-renunciation-of-protest – are justified without basic desert. However, despite the attempts made above to interpret the biblically described divine attitudes and responses to human sin in light of basic-desert moral responsibility skepticism, it is still hard to make sense of them without basic desert.

For starters, if no one is basic-desert morally responsible, it's clear why there is "no condemnation for those who are in Christ Jesus" (Romans 8:1) – but equally it would seem that there must be no condemnation for those even apart from Christ. Perhaps sin will be condemned, but sinners cannot be. And yet passages like Romans 5:18 ("just as one man's trespass led to condemnation for all, so one man's act of righteousness leads to justification and life for all") strongly suggest that divine condemnation is directed at *people*, not only their sin, just as justification is directed at people. And it is not only Paul who seems to think divine condemnation is directed at (apparently deserving) people; Jesus is reported in multiple Gospels as calling those who do not believe in Christ "condemned" (see, for instance, Mark 16:16 and John 3:18).

Similarly we can ask what it might mean, on this view, to be saved through Christ *from the wrath of God* (Romans 5:8). One might naturally take this to mean that God's wrath is destructive to the unredeemed, but through Christ the redeemed are spared this destruction. Yet on the view under consideration here, divine wrath is for the sinner's own good, since it destroys the sin which is itself destructive to the sinner. Thus being saved from divine wrath would not seem to mean entirely avoiding divine wrath, but instead, something like being preserved in the midst of it. One might find this interpretation less than intuitive, however.

Furthermore, if there is any analogy between divine wrath and human anger, then it would seem that both are directed at *persons*, and in *reaction* to something the person has done. In other words, it seems that divine wrath, like human anger, must be essentially backward-looking (or present-looking, if the person's wrongdoing is continuing). As Pamela Hieronymi similarly reasons in a review of Pereboom's recent book,

> Pereboom may hope to identify my anger as his "stance of moral protest." But that stance is forward-looking, with aims and objectives. My anger is not. It is, as Peter Strawson noted, *reactive* – it is my reaction to my perception of the quality of the [target's] will, of his practical outlook and my place within

it . . . . Whether my resentment will *accomplish* anything is, again, for better or worse, beside the point. (Hieronymi 2022)

So, too, one might think, with divine wrath. This is not to say that divine wrath does not in fact accomplish anything positive in its expression. The point, rather, is that the expression of wrath would seem appropriate only if it is deserved – unlike, say, the quarantining of an individual with a dangerous disease. In other words, its "aim and justification" must be basic desert, rather than the good that it may bring about.

Pereboom may be leery of assigning "basic-desert" moral responsibility because he assumes that basic desert, at least for blameworthy behavior, is necessarily tied to *retributive* responses, or those that involve the intentional infliction of harm or suffering for the purpose of "payback." This assumption comes out in his most recent work, in which he offers the following definition: "For an agent to be *morally responsible for an action in the basic desert sense* is for the action to be attributable to her in such a way that if she was sensitive to its being morally wrong, she would deserve to be blamed or punished in a way that she would experience as painful or harmful" (2021, 11–12). But this characterization of basic desert, I have argued, is a mistake (Vicens 2022a); for even if someone is fully morally responsible in the basic-desert sense for some wrongdoing, she may not deserve to experience any pain or harm – especially if her wrongdoing is minor. Moreover, defining basic desert this way rules out the possibility that anyone could deserve to experience reactive attitudes like anger that are not necessarily painful or harmful to their targets. Finally, if basic-desert moral responsibility is simply full-blooded moral responsibility, then no one could be morally responsible for their actions who did not have the capacity to experience pain or harm – but surely we can imagine the possibility of a person who is morally responsible for what she does, given her capacities (free will, rationality, and the like) but who is not liable to suffering. Thus basic desert should be defined without these retributive elements.

I have further argued that someone who lacks free will might still be "basic-desert" morally responsible (Vicens 2022a and forthcoming; see also Vicens 2022c). For while a lack of free will might rule out our deserving punitive responses to our immoral behavior, we may basically deserve certain treatment, including the sort of blame-as-protest that Pereboom discusses. While Pereboom thinks that protest can be justified on the grounds of the good that it may do, I have argued that it does not require any consequentialist (or contractualist) justification. For protest, even when it is expected to be futile, may be justified by appeal to its symbolic value. And such protest may be fitting and basically deserved in virtue of the fact that the target's behavior is attributable to her in the sense that it reflects her "deep self" or most fundamental attitudes and cares. Consider, for instance, a case in which a woman is raised in an authoritarian and misogynistic household and community, and comes to desire to be submissive to the men in her life, at great cost to her own well-being and happiness. We might imagine that she cannot even conceive of another option for herself, much less will it, and thus that she is not free with respect to her submissive behavior. And yet, if we suppose that the woman goes on to raise a daughter according to the values of her family and community, insisting (against the girl's wishes and best interests) that the girl similarly submit to men, it would seem that the woman is an appropriate target of protest. And it would not simply be her *behavior* that is protest-worthy, but the woman herself, and her internal attributes: her misogyny, her disrespect of the agency of her own daughter, her failure of empathy and hardness of heart in response to the obvious suffering she is causing, and so on (Vicens, forthcoming; see Hieronymi 2022 for similar sentiments).

Thus I propose that the free will skeptic allow for the possibility of basic-desert moral responsibility, while denying the possibility of retributive punishment. We might call this view "sort of" compatibilism,[43] since it lies somewhere between a full-throated affirmation that moral responsibility is compatible with determinism or a lack of the ability to do otherwise, and Pereboom-style basic-desert moral responsibility skepticism. This would allow one who concludes, based on the inevitability of sin, that we do not sin freely to make better sense of divine condemnation and wrath than the basic-desert moral responsibility skeptic can. For divine condemnation, understood as a kind of divine protest, would be deserved by all sinners whose sin is attributable to them.[44] Similarly, if divine wrath is not retributive, sinners may also be liable to it, on sort-of compatibilism. Alternatively, divine wrath might be understood as the human perception or experience of divine condemnation.[45] Sort-of compatibilism may also offer an alternative way to interpret the early Christian writers and contemporary Orthodox thinkers quoted at the beginning of this section. For instance, we might interpret Louth's claim, that the consequences of sin are amplified to

---

[43] In Vicens (2022c) I called this view a form of "responsibility revisionism," but at that point I was not committed to the idea that moral responsibility of any form cannot be divorced from basic desert.

[44] The sort-of compatibilist may still deny that divine condemnation and the like apply to infants, young children, and the cognitively disabled, to whom sin is not attributable. Such people may be said to be sinners or in need salvation from sin only in some other sense, such as being affected by *structural* sin – see, for instance, Timpe (2021). Thus, the view I am proposing here may inherit some of the bifurcation of the view considered at the beginning of this chapter. Yet on my view, divine condemnation and wrath may apply to all mature and cognitively able adults.

[45] There might be independent reason for denying that divine wrath is really intrinsic to God – for instance, if emotions are passive, and in God there is no passivity.

be more than we can be blamed for, to mean that we are deserving of blame *to some degree* for our sin, but our responsibility does not rise to the level of deserving retributive punishment.

In any case, the idea that there is no condemnation for those in Christ, or that in Christ we are saved from the wrath of God, would mean that as we are transformed into Christ's image, through the grace of God, we will no longer be deserving of divine condemnation and wrath – for sin will no longer be attributable to us. Like soft determinism and basic-desert moral responsibility skepticism, sort-of compatibilism seems least problematic on the assumption that the category of those who are *ultimately* condemned will be an empty one: God will eventually save us all from sin.

References

Adams, Marilyn McCord (1993). The Problem of Hell: A Problem of Evil for Christians. In Eleonore Stump, ed., *Reasoned Faith: Essays in Philosophical Theology in Honor of Norman Kretzmann*. Ithaca, NY: Cornell University Press, 301–327.

Adams, Marilyn McCord (1999). *Horrendous Evils and the Goodness of God*. Ithaca, NY: Cornell University Press.

Adams, Robert Merrihew (1977). Middle Knowledge and the Problem of Evil. *American Philosophical Quarterly* 14, 109–117.

Adams, Robert Merrihew (1999). *Finite and Infinite Goods: A Framework for Ethics*. New York: Oxford University Press.

Anderson, Mark (2021). On Responsibility and Original Sin: A Molinist Suggestion. *Faith and Philosophy* 38(1), 5–25.

Ayer, A. J. (1954). Freedom and Necessity. In *Philosophical Essays*, New York: St. Martin's Press: 3–20; reprinted in Watson (ed.), 1982, 15–23.

Baker, Lynne Rudder (2003). Why Christians Should Not Be Libertarians: An Augustinian Challenge. *Faith and Philosophy* 20(4), 460–478.

Burrell, David (2008). Creator/Creatures Relation: "The Distinction' v. 'Onto-theology'." *Faith and Philosophy*, 25(2), 177–189.

Byerly, T. Ryan (2017). Free Will Theodicies for Theological Determinists. *Sophia*, 56(2), 289–310.

Byrne, Peter (2008). Helm's God and the Authorship of Sin. In Martin W. F. Stone, ed., *Reason, Faith and History: Philosophical Essays for Paul Helm*. Aldershot: Ashgate, 193–203.

Capes, Justin (2022). Hard Theological Determinism and Divine Forgiveness are Incompatible. In Peter Furlong and Leigh Vicens, eds., *Theological Determinism: New Perspectives*. Cambridge: Cambridge University Press, 165–183.

Caruso, Gregg D. (2012). *Free Will and Consciousness: A Determinist Account of the Illusion of Free Will*. Lanham: Lexington Books.

Couenhoven, Jesse (2007). Augustine's Rejection of the Free-Will Defense: An Overview of the Late Augustine's Theodicy. *Religious Studies* 43(3), 279–298.

Cuneo, Terence (2016). *Ritualized Faith: Essays on the Philosophy of Liturgy*. Oxford: Oxford University Press.

Crisp, Oliver (2009). Original Sin and Atonement. In Thomas Flint and Michael Rea, eds., *The Oxford Handbook of Philosophical Theology*. Oxford: Oxford University Press, 430–451.

Crisp, Oliver (2015). On Original Sin. *International Journal of Systematic Theology* 17(3), 252–266.

Crisp, Oliver (2020). A Moderate Reformed View. In J. B. Stump and Chad Meister, eds., *Original Sin and the Fall: Five Views*. Intervarsity Press.

Demetriou, Kristen (2010). The Soft-Line Solution to Pereboom's Four-Case Argument. *Australasian Journal of Philosophy* 88, 595–617.

Ekstrom, Laura (2000). *Free Will: A Philosophical Study*. Westview Press.

Ekstrom, Laura (2021). *God, Suffering, and the Value of Free Will*. Oxford: Oxford University Press.

Finch, Alicia (2022). An Argument for Theological Incompatibilism. In Peter Furlong and Leigh Vicens, eds., *Theological Determinism: New Perspectives*. Cambridge: Cambridge University Press, 133–149.

Fischer, John Martin (1994). *The Metaphysics of Free Will: An Essay on Control*. Cambridge: Basil Blackwell.

Fischer, John Martin (2006). *My Way: Essays on Moral Responsibility*. Oxford: Oxford University Press.

Fischer, John Martin and Mark Ravizza (1998). *Responsibility and Control: A Theory of Moral Responsibility*. Cambridge: Cambridge University Press.

Flint, Thomas (1998). *Divine Providence: The Molinist Account*. Ithaca, NY: Cornell University Press.

Frankfurt, Harry (1969). Alternate Possibilities and Moral Responsibility. *Journal of Philosophy* 66, 829–839.

Frankfurt, Harry (1971). Freedom of the Will and the Concept of a Person. *Journal of Philosophy* 68, 5–20.

Franks, W. Paul (2012). Original Sin and Broad Free-Will Defense. *Philosophia Christi* 14(2), 353–371.

Freddoso, Alfred (1988). Introduction. In Alfred J. Freddoso, ed., *On Divine Foreknowledge: Part IV of the Concordia*. Ithaca, NY: Cornell University Press, 1–81.

Furlong, Peter (2019). *The Challenges of Divine Determinism: A Philosophical Analysis*. Cambridge: Cambridge University Press.

Garrard, Eve and David McNaughton (2010). *Forgiveness*. Durham: Acumen.

Grant, W. Matthews (2009). Aquinas on How God Causes the Act of Sin without Causing Sin Itself. *The Thomist* 73, 455–496.

Hasker, William (1989). *God, Time, and Knowledge*. Ithaca, NY: Cornell University Press.

Helm, Paul (1993). *The Providence of God*. Downers Grove, IL: InterVarsity Press.

Helm, Paul (2010). God, Compatibilism, and the Authorship of Sin. *Religious Studies: An International Journal for the Philosophy of Religion* 46(1), 115–124.

Hieronymi, Pamela (2001). Articulating an Uncompromising Forgiveness. *Philosophy and Phenomenological Research* 62, 529–555.

Hieronymi, Pamela (2022). Review of Derk Pereboom's *Wrongdoing and the Moral Emotions*. *Notre Dame Philosophical Reviews*. https://ndpr.nd.edu/reviews/wrongdoing-and-the-moral-emotions/#_ednref10.

Kane, Robert (2005). *A Contemporary Introduction to Free Will*. Oxford: Oxford University Press.

Levy, Neil (2011). *Hard Luck: How Luck Undermines Free Will and Moral Responsibility*. Oxford: Oxford University Press.

Louth, Andrew (2013). *Introducing Eastern Orthodox Theology*. Downers Grove, IL: InterVarsity Press.

Madueme, Hans (2021). The Theological Problem with Evolution. *Zygon*, 56 (2), 481–499.

Marshall, Christopher (2001). *Beyond Retribution: A New Testament Vision for Justice, Crime, and Punishment*. Grand Rapids, MI: Wm. B. Eerdmans.

McBrayer, Justin (2010). Skeptical Theism. *Philosophy Compass* 5(7), 611–623.

McCall, Thomas (2019). *Against God and Nature: The Doctrine of Sin*. Wheaton, IL: Crossway.

McCann, Hugh (1995). Divine Sovereignty and the Freedom of the Will. *Faith and Philosophy* 12(4), 582–598.

McCann, Hugh (2005). The Author of Sin? *Faith and Philosophy* 22(2), 144–159.

McCann, Hugh (2009). God, Sin, and Rogers on Anselm: A Reply. *Faith and Philosophy* 26(4), 420–431.

McCann, Hugh and Daniel Johnson (2017). Divine Providence. In Edward N. Zalta and Uri Nodelman, eds., *Stanford Encyclopedia of Philosophy*, https://plato.stanford.edu/archives/win2022/entries/providence-divine/.

McKenna, Michael (2008). A Hard-line Reply to Pereboom's Four-Case Manipulation Argument. *Philosophy and Phenomenological Research* 77(1), 142–159.

Mele, Alfred (2006). *Free Will and Luck*. Oxford: Oxford University Press.

Moo, Douglas (2013). Sin in Paul. In Christopher Morgan and Robert Peterson, eds., *Fallen: A Theology of Sin*. Wheaton, IL: Crossway, 107–130.

Morgan, Christopher (2013). Sin in the Biblical Story. In Christopher Morgan and Robert Peterson, eds., *Fallen: A Theology of Sin*. Wheaton, IL: Crossway, 131–162.

Nahmias, Eddy, and Dylan Murray (2010). Experimental Philosophy on Free Will: An Error Theory for Incompatibilist Intuitions. In Jesus Aguilar,

Andrei Buckareff, and Keith Frankish, eds., *New Waves in Philosophy of Action*. London: Palgrave-Macmillan, 189–215.

O'Connor, Timothy (1995). Agent Causation. Reprinted in Gary Watson, ed., *Free Will: Second Edition* (2003). Oxford: Oxford University Press, 257–284.

O'Connor, Timothy (2016). Against Theological Determinism. In Kevin Timpe and Daniel Speak, eds., *Free Will and Theism: Connections, Contingencies, and Concerns*. Oxford: Oxford University Press, 132–141.

Pereboom, Derk (2001). *Living without Free Will*. Cambridge: Cambridge University Press.

Pereboom, Derk (2014). *Free Will, Agency, and Meaning in Life*. Oxford: Oxford University Press.

Pereboom, Derk (2016). Libertarianism and Theological Determinism. In Kevin Timpe and Daniel Speak, eds., *Free Will and Theism: Connections, Contingencies, and Concerns*. Oxford: Oxford University Press, 112–129.

Pereboom, Derk (2017). Responsibility, Regret, and Protest. In David Shoemaker, ed., *Oxford Studies in Agency and Responsibility, Vol. 4*, 121–140. Oxford: Oxford University Press.

Pereboom, Derk (2021). *Wrongdoing and the Moral Emotions*. Oxford: Oxford University Press.

Plantinga, Alvin (1974). *The Nature of Necessity*. New York: Clarendon Press.

Plantinga, Cornelius (1995). *Not the Way It's Supposed to Be: A Breviary of Sin*. Grand Rapids, MI: William B. Eerdmans.

Pruss, Alexander (2016). The First Sin: A Dilemma for Christian Determinists. In David E. Alexander and Daniel M. Johnson, eds., *Calvinism and the Problem of Evil*. Eugene, OR: Pickwick, 187–199.

Quinn, Philip (2010). Sin and Original Sin. In Charles Taliaferro, Paul Draper, and Philip Quinn, eds., *A Companion to Philosophy of Religion*, 2nd ed., Blackwell, 614–621. West Sussex.

Rea, Michael (2007). The Metaphysics of Original Sin. In Dean Zimmerman, ed., *Persons: Human and Divine*. Oxford: Oxford University Press, 319–356.

Rhoda, Alan (2010). Gratuitous Evil and Divine Providence. *Religious Studies*, 46(3), 281–302.

Rogers, Katherin (2002). The Abolition of Sin: A Response to Adams in the Augustinian Tradition. *Faith and Philosophy* 19(1), 69–84.

Rogers, Katherin (2007). God is Not the Author of Sin: An Anselmian Response to McCann. *Faith and Philosophy* 24(3), 300–310.

Rogers, Katherin A. (2011). Anselm against McCann on God and Sin: Further Discussion. *Faith and Philosophy* 28(4), 397–415.

Searle, John (1984). *Minds, Brains, and Science.* Cambridge, MA: Harvard University Press.

Strabbing, Jada (2017). Divine Forgiveness and Reconciliation. *Faith and Philosophy* 34(3), 272–297.

Strawson, Peter F. (1963). Freedom and Resentment. Reprinted in Gary Watson. ed., *Free Will*, 2nd ed. (2003). Oxford: Oxford University Press.

Strawson, Peter (1994). The Impossibility of Moral Responsibility. *Philosophical Studies* 75(1–2), 5–24.

Stump, Eleonore (1985). The Problem of Evil. *Faith and Philosophy* 2(4), 392–423.

Stump, Eleonore (1988). Sanctification, Hardening of the Heart, and Frankfurt's Concept of Free Will. *The Journal of Philosophy* 85(8), 395–420.

Stump, Eleonore (2008). The Problem of Evil and the Desires of the Heart. In Michael Rea and Louis Pojman, eds., *Philosophy of Religion: An Anthology.* Cengage, 338–350.

Swenson, Philip (2021). Equal Moral Opportunity: A Solution to the Problem of Moral Luck. *Australian Journal of Philosophy* 100(2), 386–404.

Swinburne, Richard (1989). *Responsibility and Atonement.* New York: Clarendon Press.

Talbott, Thomas (1999). *The Inescapable Love of God.* Universal Publishers.

Talbott, Thomas (2008). Why Christians Should not be Determinists: Reflections on the Origin of Human Sin. *Faith and Philosophy* 25(3), 300–316.

Tanner, Kathryn. (1994). Human Freedom, Human Sin, and God the Creator. In T. Tracy, ed., *The God Who Acts: Philosophical and Theological Explorations.* University Park: Pennsylvania State University Press, 111–135.

Timpe, Kevin (2007). Source Incompatibilism and Its Alternatives. *American Philosophical Quarterly* 44(2), 143–155.

Timpe, Kevin (2021). Sin in Christian Thought. In Edward N. Zalta, ed., *The Stanford Encyclopedia of Philosophy.* https://plato.stanford.edu/archives/win2021/entries/sin-christian/.

Todd, Patrick (2012). Manipulation and Moral Standing. *Philosophers' Imprint* 12(7), 1–18.

Tognazzini, Neil (2011). Understanding Source Incompatibilism. *The Modern Schoolman* 88(1–2), 73–88.

Van Inwagen, Peter (1983). *An Essay on Free Will.* Oxford: Oxford University Press.

Van Inwagen, Peter (2008). How to Think about the Problem of Free Will. *The Journal of Ethics* 12, 327–341.

Vicens, Leigh (2012a). *Divine Determinism: A Critical Consideration.* PhD Dissertation, University of Wisconsin-Madison.https://depot.library.wisc.edu/repository/fedora/1711.dl:YABHRJWC6G4NO8I/datastreams/REF/content

Vicens, Leigh (2012b). Divine Determinism, Human Freedom, and the Consequence Argument. *International Journal for Philosophy of Religion* 71, 145–155.

Vicens, Leigh (2014). Theological Determinism. *Internet Encyclopedia of Philosophy.* https://iep.utm.edu/theo-det/.

Vicens, Leigh (2018). Sin and Implicit Bias. *Journal of Analytic Theology* 6, 100–111.

Vicens, Leigh (2022a). Free Will Skeptics Can Have their Basic Desert and Eat It Too. *Journal of the American Philosophical Association*, 1–12. www .cambridge.org/core/journals/journal-of-the-american-philosophical-associ ation/article/abs/free-will-skeptics-can-have-their-basic-desert-and-eat-it-too/DF94843190B570B6119537F0C64FA587.

Vicens, Leigh (2022b). Human Freedom and the Inevitability of Sin. In Peter Furlong and Leigh Vicens, eds., *Theological Determinism: New Perspectives* 150–164. Cambridge: Cambridge University Press.

Vicens, Leigh (2022c). Sin and the Faces of Responsibility. In John Allan Knight and Ian Markham, eds., *The Craft of Innovative Theology: Argument & Practice.* Wiley Blackwell, 99–113 Hoboken, NJ.

Vicens, Leigh (forthcoming). Can the Unfree Person Have a Deep Self? In Aku Visala and Olli-Pekka Vainio, eds., *Theological Perspectives on Free Will: Compatibility, Christology, Community.* Routledge.

Vicens, Leigh and Simon Kittle (2019). *God and Human Freedom.* Cambridge University Press.

Visala, Aku (2021). How the Cognitive Sciences Might Contribute to the Theological Debate about Free Will. *Modern Theology* 37(2), 362–381.

Visala, Aku and Olli-Pekka Vainio (2020). Erasmus versus Luther: A Contemporary Analysis of the Debate on Free Will. *Neue Zeitschrift für systematische Theologie und Religionsphilosophie* 62(3), 311–335.

Warmke, Brandon, Dana Kay Nelkin, and Michael McKenna (2021). *Forgiveness and its Moral Dimensions.* Oxford: Oxford University Press.

Watson, Gary (1975). Free Agency. *Journal of Philosophy* 72(8), 205–220.

White, Heath (2016). Theological Determinism and the "Authoring of Sin" Objection. In David Alexander and Daniel Johnson, eds., *Calvinism and the Problem of Evil.* Eugene, OR: Wipf and Stock, 78–95.

Witherington III, Ben (2005). *The Problem with Evangelical Theology: Testing the Exegetical Foundations of Calvinism, Dispensationalism, and Wesleyanism.* Waco, TX: Baylor University Press.

Wolf, Susan (1990). *Freedom within Reason.* Oxford: Oxford University Press.

Yandell, Keith (1999). *Philosophy of Religion: A Contemporary Introduction.* New York: Routledge.

Acknowledgments

Many thanks to those who read through drafts of these sections: Taylor Cyr, Peter Furlong, Derk Pereboom, Mike Rea, Kevin Timpe, Aku Visala, and Heath White.

The Problems of God

Printed in the United States
by Baker & Taylor Publisher Services